ADVANCED PRAISE FOR SMALL BUSINESS HACKS

"What Moltz and Lesonsky have put together is a must have book for your small business. Even if you've launched, go back and read this. There's meat here."

- Chris Brogan, Business Advisor and Author.

"This should be required reading for every small business. You can save so much heartache and money by applying even a few of these hacks. And, it's an easy read to boot! Grab your copy today."

- Shama Hyder, CEO of Marketing Zen and Best-Selling Author of The Zen of Social Media Marketing (4th edition)

"Most small business owners have no idea what it takes to run a business. Well look no further than these 100 hacks for success"

- Mike Michalowicz, Author of Profit First

small business hacks

100
SHORTCUTS TO SUCCESS

BARRY MOLTZ
RIEVA LESONSKY

LEADERS IN GLOBAL PUBLISHING

Published by Motivational Press, Inc.
1777 Aurora Road
Melbourne, Florida, 32935
www.MotivationalPress.com

Manufactured in the United States of America.

ISBN: 978-1-62865-443-1

CONTENTS

MANAGEMENT HACKS 52

TECHNOLOGY HACKS 88

From Barry

My parents, Alan and Carole taught me that there were no shortcuts…until you had done the work the first time to learn what those shortcuts were.

From Rieva

To my father, grandfathers and uncle who taught me the "secrets" of small business, and that the best shortcut to success is knowing your customers and practicing the "Golden Rule."

ACKNOWLEDGEMENTS

From Barry

Rieva Lesonsky for being my mentor and co-author on this book. She always imparts her wisdom that guides me to do the right thing.

The small business owners I meet and talk to every week that teach me that taking action is the real key to success.

Sara Shafran, my spouse who has been my traveling companion for 26 years along with my sons, Ethan and Daniel.

Michael Port who first taught me how valuable hacks can be.

JJ Ramberg for having the longest running small business show on any network (and writing the preface!).

To all the small business owners that contributed their valuable and tough-fought knowledge in the form of hacks for this book

My Seido Karate teachers, Shihans Nancy Lanoue and Sarah Ludden, who teach me to face fear and go ahead anyways. Osu!

From Rieva

I wouldn't be here without the help, guidance and support of a lot of people. I truly believe it took a village to raise me.

My village:

Mrs. Healy, the librarian at Sunquam Elementary School, who let me check out as many books as I wanted to read every week, encouraging my love of words.

Mr. Strickland, my 6th grade teacher at Sunquam, Mr. Monner, my social studies teacher at Burr's Lane Junior High and Mr. Alford, my 11th –grade English teacher at Half Hollow Hills HS, who all encouraged me to think, talk and write outside the proverbial box. And my guidance counselor, who kept insisting I become a teacher, until I told him I wanted to be a journalist, because I couldn't think of anything else to say.

A counselor at camp who "made" me write the camp newsletter, my first "professional" writing gig.

Journalists who have informed and inspired me since I was 12.

George Murray, who hired me on the spot, at *Entrepreneur* magazine, long before most people knew what an entrepreneur was—or did.

Barry Moltz, who "made" me write this book with him.

Fred DeLuca, founder of Subway Sandwiches, who showed me no matter how rich and successful you become, you should never be an asshat.

My parents, Mimi & Jerry Lesonsky, who encouraged me to become whatever I wanted. I learned how to "march to the beat of my own drum" because of them. I miss you every day Daddy.

My siblings Ron, Robin and Jayne, who allowed me to develop and practice my management skills. Being your big sister was the best training one could ask for.

Maria Anton, Maria Haubrich and Karen Axelton for being there.

The "kids": Cassie, Ricky, Danielle, Zach, Elleni, Julianna and Alexandra for giving me hope the future is in good hands.

Skip Brendmoen, my partner in life, who loves, coaches, encourages and takes care of me every day. I couldn't do any of it without him.

The millions of small business owners and entrepreneurs who have let me into their lives for more than 30 years. It is because of you my personal motto has become, "If you believe, and if you persist—all things are possible."

FOREWORD

THERE ARE ONLY 24 HOURS in a day. For many of us running small businesses, that's about 24 hours too few. I often daydream about what more I could accomplish if I simply had more time. But the truth is, I could have more time. We all could. We are all guilty of spending too much time getting certain things done.

For the past 11 years, I have been hosting the program *Your Business* on MSNBC for which I've interviewed thousands of successful small business owners. At the same time, I've been growing my own company— Goodshop—which I founded with my brother in 2005. What I've learned from both experiences is that the majority of what we do as business owners has already been done by someone else. And, we can buy back hours and hours of time by simply finding out how they did it, rather than starting from scratch ourselves. While creativity and innovation are necessary for some parts of our businesses, for others, there is no need to reinvent the wheel.

And that's where this book comes in. I met Rieva Lesonsky more than a decade ago when she was a guest on a program I hosted for CNNfn and she was the editorial director of *Entrepreneur* Magazine. Barry and I have gotten to know each other through *Your Business*. Over the years, both of them have given thoughtful advice to my audiences about how to shorten tasks that, at first glance, seem like they'll take up a lot of your precious time. In *Small Business Hacks*, they have compiled all this advice into one easy-to-find place. Chances are, no matter what you need to do to help grow your business, you'll find a hack in here to help you.

JJ Ramberg
Host, MSNBC's *Your Business*
Cofounder, Goodshop.com

INTRODUCTION

R UNNING A SMALL BUSINESS can be hard, confusing and mysterious. Many entrepreneurs start a company to solve a problem, and want to focus on doing just that. Unfortunately, there are a lot of aspects of starting and running a business that seem to get in the way of that pursuit, such as:

» Marketing and selling your products or services

» Providing an outstanding customer experience

» Leading and managing employees, freelancers and vendors

» Managing your finances.

This book solves those problems—and many more.

Small Business Hacks is a simple guide for current and aspiring business owners. It's intended to take the mystery out of small business ownership, to show you how to accomplish tasks in as few steps as possible, to relieve the angst over searching for the right solution on the web. These 100 small business hacks are truly your shortcut to success.

These hacks are from our combined 50+ years in business both as small business owners and as journalists interviewing successful entrepreneurs and thought leaders about their paths to prosperity. We also tapped the best industry experts to fill in any gaps.

It has never been easier to start a business, but with so much competition all over the world, it's also easy to fail.

Small Business Hacks is not a traditional book—it's not meant to be read from beginning to end. Instead, it's built for immediate action. Jump to the challenge you're currently facing, and find out how to solve it—now!

Keep this guide handy. It gives you immediate access to solutions you can quickly enact, which gives you more time to do what you love at your company.

We realize not every problem can be solved in an instant. For those, we've listed additional resources at the end of each hack, so you can get more information.

We wrote this book to make your entrepreneurial journey smoother. We hope we've accomplished that. If you have a hack or shortcut you want to share with other small business owners, please connect with us at www.yoursmallbizhacks.com. And we wish you the best of luck on your journey.

Barry Moltz
www.barrymoltz.com

Rieva Lesonsky Rieva
@SmallBizDaily.com

STARTUP
HACKS

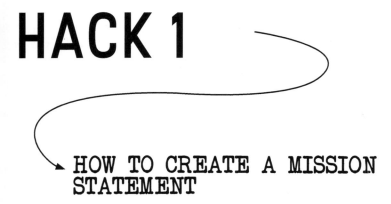

HOW TO CREATE A MISSION STATEMENT

MANY ASPIRING SMALL BUSINESS owners conflate defining a vision for their businesses and developing a mission statement. But those are two different, though important, elements of creating a solid foundation for your business.

Your company's vision, says Tim Berry, founder of Palo Alto Software, is essentially a future forecast. He advises entrepreneurs to "Imagine what your company should be (its size, its business offerings, its customers, and so forth) three years from now. That's your vision." Obviously as your business grows, your vision should evolve.

Your mission statement encapsulates your goals, philosophies, objectives and how you intend to serve your customers and employees. Who is a mission statement written for? You, to begin with. Just the act of creating it will help you clarify why you're in business. But it's also vitally important for your employees to understand your company's mission and the part they play in it.

To come up with a mission statement that truly reflects your business, ask yourself some questions:

- » Why did you start/buy this business?
- » Who are your customers?
- » What do you stand for?
- » What perception do you want others to have of your company?

» What are you selling?

» What kind of work environment have you created?

» What sets you apart from your competition?

While a mission statement should be short—no longer than three or so paragraphs, it should not be slapped together or created in haste. Take your time and get input from people you trust, whether they be members of your team, friends, family, your accountant or your lawyer. This is important, even if you are a solo entrepreneur. We're all familiar with the cliché, "Can't see the forest for the trees." That is a particularly apt expression for business owners who are so close to their ideas, it's all too easy to overlook the obvious. Your mission statement will be better if you have someone challenge you on it—and try to defend your assertions.

If you're stuck creating your mission statement, look at the ones other companies have created. (Don't copy; use these for inspiration.)

Once you're done make sure your employees understand your company's mission. If you like, you can post your mission statement in your store/office/restaurant/facility and on your website so your customers can see it.

Like business plans, mission statements shouldn't be written and forgotten. Periodically review your mission statement to make sure it still reflects your operating philosophy and, if it does, to ensure your actions support the mission. If you've outgrown your original mission, create a new one that signifies your new goals.

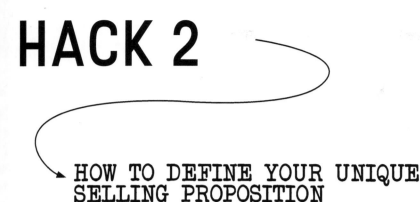

HACK 2

HOW TO DEFINE YOUR UNIQUE SELLING PROPOSITION

EVERY SMALL BUSINESS needs to define, understand and live its unique selling proposition (USP). A USP is exactly what it sounds like, it's what makes your business different—makes it stand out from the crowd.

How can you best determine your USP?

1—USPs are about benefits, not features. How does your business help your customers and clients? What's the benefit to them of doing business with you? For instance, a green cleaning service reduces the risk of your customers' families being exposed to allergens.

2—The four Ps of marketing. Think about how the four Ps—product, price, placement (distribution channels) and promotional methods, and how they can help you define what's special about your small business. Do you sell hard-to-find products? Are your products organic? Is your service green? Do you donate a portion of profits to charity?

3—Do you know why your customers do business with you? Understanding this will help you craft an effective USP. To find out—ask them. Conduct a survey or poll (this is easy and cheap to do online) or ask them in person. You can have an informal focus group, or just take some of your loyal customers out to lunch to get their insights. Monitor social media and ratings and review sites to see what people are saying online.

Are your clients and customers looking to reaffirm their values, to get a good deal, to protect their loved ones, etc.?

4—Be emotional. Once you discover why your customers buy from you, use that information and add some emotion to your USP—it will help your audience connect to you and forge customer loyalty.

5—What are your competitors' USPs? If you're trying to stand out from the pack, you need to know how your competition defines themselves. You should always monitor your prime competition. Check their physical locations, website, social platforms and marketing messages to help you determine what they stand for and how you can differentiate your business. By definition, a USP that is "shared" by others is not unique. For instance, think about Domino's Pizza. Its USP was *not* that they delivered pizza. It was the guarantee that you'd get your pizza in 30 minutes or less or you'd get you money back. That USP was truly unique—and helped create a multi-billion-dollar company.

Once you create your USP, you need to make sure your business lives it. Think of your USP as a promise you're making to your customers—and nothing will drive business away faster than broken promises.

Don't make the mistake of thinking you only need to worry about your USP at startup. As your business—or the market—evolves, you should reassess your USP to make sure it still reflects your small business.

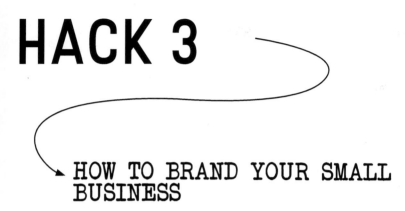

HACK 3

HOW TO BRAND YOUR SMALL BUSINESS

BUILDING A BRAND is not the first thing entrepreneurs should do. Before you create a brand, you need to name your business, register your website, design a logo, develop your mission and vision statements and determine your USP. Only then can you start creating your brand.

Branding your business has nothing to do with marketing or advertising, although you will use marketing and advertising to build your brand. Your brand reflects the "personality" of your business—the feeling you want to evoke in prospective customers when they think about your company. Is your brand homespun or sophisticated, all-American or exotic, cutting-edge or retro?

To define your brand, you might want to refer to your mission statement (Hack #1). You should be able to summarize what your brand stands for in one sentence. For example, "Helping Hands is the in-home care service that provides seniors with friendly care, and their loved ones with peace of mind."

It's important to share your brand identity with your employees (if you have any) or contract workers, since they're likely to be the ones conveying your brand message to customers.

Promoting a consistent visual identity is key to building your brand. Your visual identity stems from your logo, which should appear on all your marketing and advertising materials, from employee uniforms to your business cards and, of course, your business website, product packaging, signage and ads.

However, your visual identity goes far beyond your logo. Your marketing materials—such as signage, uniforms or restaurant décor—should use the same colors, style and graphics of your logo. Using consistent visual elements in all your marketing materials will condition customers to associate these elements with your brand.

Social media offers a whole new way to expand your brand. Create social media accounts for your brand, using your logo and any other visual elements that identify your brand. Then share and post content that reflects your brand identity. For example, if your brand is snarky and humorous, you might post funny memes or GIFs—but that wouldn't be appropriate for a home healthcare business, for example. For that type of business, sharing informational articles or resource links about senior care would make more sense. When in doubt, think back to the personality concept: when posting anything, consider whether it reflects your brand's personality.

Most important, make sure *you* are living your brand values. Does the way you act and the things you do reflect your brand? For the home healthcare business, for instance, getting involved with community organizations that help seniors, participating in senior-related or health-related community events, or contributing to charitable organizations can all help to build your brand image.

It doesn't have to cost a fortune to build a business brand. Something as simple as including your logo at the bottom of every email you send can make a difference in cementing your brand in customers' minds. The key to brand building success is being consistent, and that's something every business can do.

HACK 4

HOW TO OPEN A BUSINESS BANK ACCOUNT

By Liz Romero, SVP, Small Business Central Division Executive, Bank of America

ONGRATS! YOU'VE DECIDED to fulfill your dreams and become a business owner. Now, one of the first steps you could take is to open a business banking account. For background, businesses that are corporations or limited liability companies (LLC) are well advised by law to have business finances that are separate from the owners' personal accounts. Even if you're a sole proprietor, though, it's wise to keep your personal and business accounts separate for easier money management and tax reporting.

As you consider your banking needs and options, keep in mind the structure of business accounts differs from that of personal bank accounts, as does the process for applying. Here are steps I recommend to help you evaluate your choices and prepare for the application process.

1—Compare your options: Business bank accounts range from those providing basic banking services to those servicing more complex business needs or enabling sales transactions. Here are some things to keep in mind when examining the different offers and options:

» **Fees:** Since business checking accounts often involve larger, more frequent deposits, the fees charged differ from those of personal accounts so you'll want to compare fees closely to understand how they are structured, including:

» **Activity limits:** Will your business make a high number or high dollar amount of transactions? If so, you could closely compare how monthly activity limits could impact you.

» **Maintenance fees:** Some accounts require a minimum monthly balance to avoid a monthly fee. If your business maintains a steady cash flow and doesn't dip below a certain predictable level, a checking account with a minimum balance requirement will probably save you money.

» **Automated Clearing House (ACH) transfers:** Will you need to transfer money between accounts frequently? If so, look for a bank account that allows free ACH transfers.

» **Interest checking:** Some business accounts earn interest. Compare rates and requirements to see if you can earn a little extra cash through your account.

» **Merchant accounts:** Also, it's important to decide early on if your business will need to accept debit and credit card sales. If the answer is yes, you could consider getting a merchant account that enables businesses to accept these sales (usually for a fee).

» **Online/mobile banking:** Online banking is a convenient way to stay current on your account balance from anywhere. Try looking for accounts that offer features like low-balance alerts, transaction notices, online bill pay and mobile check deposit.

» **Account management tools:** Ask your bank about the account management solutions they provide, such as an integration with QuickBooks or another platform that can help with account management productivity.

2—Consider future needs: While setting your business account up is an immediate priority, don't forget to think about the long game and how your needs may change as your business grows. Will you need an expansion loan? Help handling payroll? Consider looking for banks that understand your industry and can meet those future needs.

3—Organize and apply: Now that you've completed all the research and decided what account is best, it's time to gather the necessary information and paperwork and apply. Depending on the bank or type of account, you may need:

» Business documentation such as filing documents, organizing documents, articles of incorporation and/or certificate of resolution

» Your business Tax ID

» The name and address of your business

» The date your business was established

» The state in which your business was formed

» The state in which your business operates

» Your SSN, address and DOB, and that of any of other owners

Finally, know that you don't need to navigate your finances on your own. Your bank is a resource to help guide you through the process and help set you up for success, so if you are ever unsure or have questions, don't hesitate to consult with a small business banker. That's what we're here for!

Bank of America, N.A. provides informational reading materials for your discussion or review purposes only. Interpretations in this release are not intended, nor implied, to be a substitute for the professional advice received from a qualified accountant, attorney or financial advisor. Neither Bank of America, its affiliates, nor their employees provide legal, accounting and tax advice.

HACK 5

HOW LEAN BUSINESS PLANNING WORKS

By Sabrina Parsons, CEO, Palo Alto Software

THESE DAYS, MORE THAN EVER, as a business owner and entrepreneur, you need to innovate or die. This mantra is especially true for any business in the technology sector. We constantly need to move forward, create new things, better and faster. The pressure a small business owner feels to leverage innovation into growth is only emphasized by how quickly technology marches forward, and how much every company is forced to adopt technology and innovate to keep up with the competition. So how do you keep innovating? How do you build a team and foster the right culture to help your company stay on track, and focus on building and innovating to keep growing and moving forward?

After 10 years of being CEO of Palo Alto Software, and over 20 years in the startup and entrepreneurial world, I am convinced that the only way to grow your company as quickly as possible, while not getting ulcers, becoming an insomniac, and aging more than your years, is to engage in Lean Planning and Management. Lean planning leads to lean management, and is the answer for anyone who has ever said, "I don't plan because it takes too much time, and a few months down the road my plans change—it's just not worth the time." If you run a business and have ever said something like this—Lean Planning and Management is for you. So now…. what is it, and how do you do it?

Lean Planning and Management is not a product, or a service, it is a methodology, a way of managing your business. It is about understanding the minimum viable planning you must engage in, and how to manage your business to that plan in order to grow your business strategically. It is a methodology that allows you to make decisions about what opportunities to take, and which ones to ignore.

What does a Lean Plan look like? It should have:

» An executive summary, or pitch, preferably with charts and images to tell your story quickly and efficiently

» A financial plan with a projected Sales Forecast, Profit & Loss, Cash Flow Forecast, and Balance Sheet

» An action plan with milestones scheduled and accountability baked in

» Performance tracking to compare *actual* financial results with your planned financials and other key metrics

By creating a Lean Plan, regularly reviewing it, and managing your results against that plan, you will have more clarity in decision making, and will be better positioned to quickly make the right decisions that will drive the growth you are seeking.

Sabrina Parsons is CEO of Palo Alto Software, developer of the best-selling business management software, LivePlan. A graduate of Princeton University, Sabrina assumed the CEO role in May 2007 and is responsible for Palo Alto's business planning, fiscal and strategic goals and all of the company's traditional marketing.

Resource

Palo Alto Software: http://www.paloalto.com/
Lean Business Planning: http://leanplan.com/

HACK 6

HOW MUCH MONEY DO YOU NEED TO START A BUSINESS?

By Hal Shelton, SCORE Mentor,
Angel Investor & Bestselling Author

E stimating the cost of starting your own business is critical since you will devote all your time and most of your resources to making it a success. You need to know, upfront, that this idea has the likelihood of being economically viable. Also, if you obtain a loan, you will probably provide a personal guarantee; so, if you initially did not ask for sufficient funding, you might have few resources remaining to support a second borrowing.

Estimating the amount of capital needed to start a business results from your business planning. Estimating the costs for each step in your business creation is a logical approach supported by your action plans, and it is much simpler than staring at a long list of expenditures and trying to pull numbers out of the air. The recommended approach is fully described in my book *The Secrets of Writing a Successful Business Plan*. Here are some of the startup costs you'll need to estimate during the first six months of operation.

1—What product or service are you offering to customers?

» What activities are needed to offer the product/service in a condition sufficient to start the business and what will it cost to get there? It is helpful to develop a product development road map for describing the increasing maturity of your product or service.

» For example, if you have a store, you probably have nothing to start with, but need a fully functioning facility on opening day. If you are creating an e-commerce business, a minimum viable product might be acceptable to start with subsequent and continuous enhancements. If you are starting a home-based consulting business you might have just marketing activities/expenses at startup.

2—What is the production setup if this is a manufactured product, or supply chain if you have a purchase for resale business?

» What facilities, tooling, inventory, staffing, licensing, rents, permits, quality control/testing, etc. are necessary to have this production? And how much will each cost?

3—What is the go-to-market strategy?

» How will you identify customers, get leads and close sales? Will you have an in-house sales team, use channel partners or distributors or some combination. What is the sales team staffing compensation (salary/commission) and when is the sales team needed relative to when product/service is available?

» What third-party resources will you be using—advertising, PR, lead generation, proposal writing?

» Do you need a CRM, website or other systems? What about trade shows?

4—What is the company's administrative infrastructure?

» Where is the office and what are the associated costs, such as rent, utilities, furniture, computers, printers, etc.?

» What is the staffing and their compensation/benefits—will they be employees or contractors?

» What systems are needed, such as payroll, accounting, billing, etc. and programs, such as insurance?

» Do you need third-party assistance, such as a lawyer for setting up the company or writing contracts, an accountant for bookkeeping and payroll?

5—Contingency

Starting a business is difficult and it rarely goes exactly as planned, so provide a contingency in the range of 10-25% to provide a cushion for unknown events and the extra time startup might take.

Map out the key activities necessary to implement and operate your business idea for six months and estimate the cost for each—which is all part of the business planning process. This is the amount of funding you will need from yourself, partners, family and friends or other sources like banks, crowdfunding or angels to successfully launch your business idea.

Hal Shelton is a SCORE mentor, active angel investor and author of Amazon best seller, The Secrets to Writing a Successful Business Plan; *all after having been a successful CFO/Board member for publicly traded companies and non-profits. Hal is using his knowledge and expertise to help entrepreneurs start, grow and in some cases, sell their businesses.*

RESOURCE

The Secrets of Writing a Successful Business Plan: https://www.amazon.com/Secrets-Writing-Successful-Business-Step/dp/0989946002

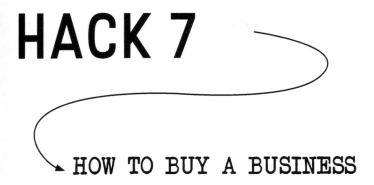

HACK 7

HOW TO BUY A BUSINESS

By Luba Kagan, Strategic Partners Manager, BizBuySell.com

ENTREPRENEURSHIP AND STARTING your own business has become quite sexy and glamorous these days, but the research shows that between 60 and 90% of startup businesses fail within five years and most startups fail within the first two years. Yet, if you buy an existing business, instead of starting from scratch, you have a much better chance of succeeding as an entrepreneur.

Start by finding the right small business to buy by searching online market places such as BizBuySell.com, BizQuest.com, and others. You can also source prospects by using business brokers from professional organizations, such as IBBA.org or local business broker associations such as CABB.org (California), NEBBA.org (North East), etc. Or try sourcing directly For Sale By Owner (FSBO) opportunities.

As you search for a business to buy remember: The heart of the search process is *learn, filter, and ask more questions*. It's an iterative process. Below are initial filters/questions to keep in mind:

» Is it an established business, or a startup or turnaround?

» Is it the right size range?

» Is it located in a place you are willing to live?

» Do you have skills to manage it?

» Does it fit your lifestyle?

» Do the earnings of the business provide you an acceptable living?

» Why is the seller selling the business?

After you identified some businesses of interest to you call or email the broker for more information. If you're still interested, go see the broker and the business (confidentially). Then meet with the seller (take the broker with you) and ask more questions. Evaluate whether the business works for you and your family based on your initial assessment.

> *Pro Tip: At this stage, you are trying to learn just enough to eliminate based on initial filters. You cannot learn everything right now—it's preliminary due diligence. My favorite analogy is: You have to go on many dates before you get married. Go see businesses, learn, evaluate and keep moving. The first business you 'meet' may or may not be the one you 'fall in love' with and buy.*

Here are some deeper filters I use to evaluate businesses. These filters help assess the enduring profitability of a business:

» Does the business have a strong reputation?

» Does it have strong competitors?

» Does it have a solid, established customer base?

» Does the business have recurring customers/revenue?

» Do the company's top five customers account for a lot of its revenue?

» Does it have fragmented customers & suppliers?

» Is year-to-year sales growth coming from the right places?

» Are sales seasonal? Does it have steady sales?

> ### Pro Tip: Small Business Buying Tips:
>
> *1. Focus on the business, not just the financials: The financials of the business have been done to minimize taxes, not to show earnings!*

2. *Focus on the top line, not the bottom line: Sales drive value—if you don't have sales, you don't have a business. My rule of thumb: earnings should be 10-20% of sales.*

3. *Focus on what you are going to do with the business: 70% of your focus should be on what improvements you can make to the business and 30% of your focus should be on what the seller has done with the business.*

If the business has been around at least three to five years, the seller has obviously been making a living from the business.

Making an offer is just the start of your due diligence and negotiation, but you need to make one to arrive at price, terms and conditions. The offer should be at a price you feel comfortable with, subject to due diligence. Best practices are a written offer, with a $1,000 refundable good faith deposit. When making your initial offer, note that most small businesses sell at about 50-60% of gross sales and 2-2.5x multiple of earnings.

The offer should include a down payment you can write a check for. Remember, as a buyer you'll need cash for the down payment, your working capital needs and enough money to live on after paying the debt service.

See what the seller responds with in writing. They may want a larger down payment or a shorter period.

Then the final due diligence begins. You should:

» Hire a CPA to help verify financial information
» Verify earnings: i.e., look at tax returns, P&Ls, bank statements
» Verify seller's representation of gross sales
» Verify seller's representation of owner's benefit
» Verify in-place contracts and obligations and customer mix
» Verify an acceptable lease transfer, industry non-compete, and training and transition period for new management
» Verify normal level of inventory

» Verify all equipment is in working order

Once you are ready to close the purchase and take ownership, the seller must make reps and warranties of the completeness of the information they've given you. If the seller is helping finance the purchase (as many as 90% of businesses sold are financed, at least in part, by the seller), that helps validate their reps and warranties.

Luba Kagan is Strategic Partners Manager at BizBuySell, the largest and most active businesses for sale marketplace.

RESOURCE

BizBuySell: http://www.bizbuysell.com/

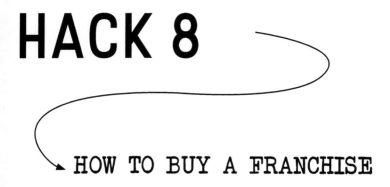

HACK 8

HOW TO BUY A FRANCHISE

By Joel Libava, The Franchise King

IT'S BEEN SUGGESTED THAT the franchise business model is the best business model ever developed. I happen to agree. But to fully leverage its greatness—to become a successful franchise business owner—you need to work through a very specific step-by-step process.

You can do this in a relatively short period of time. The steps are below—just don't skip any of them!

The four steps to take:

1—Getting started. This step will save you a lot of time.

As much as you're tempted to start visiting franchise opportunity websites to search for franchises to buy right out of gate—don't. It's a huge waste of time. Instead, you need to start the process with an "inner" search. Do these 2 things:

» Make sure you are wired correctly for franchise business ownership.

By "wired" I'm referring to your ability (and desire) to follow all the rules. For instance, are you known to be a rule-follower, or do you prefer to get somewhat "creative" with them? When you're handed a 300-page franchise operating manual at headquarters, will you be committed to follow it to a T? These questions are important, so if you have some doubt, you should rethink franchising.

» Write a list of what you feel are your five-star professional skills.

For example, do you excel at marketing? Are you a terrific operations person?

Whatever you wrote down, think about the types of businesses that could best utilize those skills. Once you've done that, you can start looking for a franchise opportunity that may match those skills.

2—Combine your search with your budget. How disappointed would you be if you found what you thought was the "perfect" franchise, only to discover that it was totally unaffordable? The best way to avoid that scenario is by taking a personal financial snapshot. Here's how: Do a net worth statement so you can determine things like assets, debt and liquid capital.

> **Pro Tip:** *Use your favorite search engine to find a free net worth calculator. Or you can use the free calendar on my site: The FranchiseKing.com.*

Once you've found out where you stand financially, you can start searching in earnest for the right franchise—and one you can afford.

3—Contact franchisors. Once you've come up with a few franchise options, you need to reach out to the franchise development representative (franchise salespeople).

Warning: This step is a (*gulp*) difficult one. It's where most people stop. This is where fear sets in. Typical self-talk at this point can include:

"What the heck am I doing?"

"This is crazy! I need to go find a job!"

"I can't afford to lose this kind of money."

And so on.

If this happens to you, I encourage you to find a way to walk through the fear. There's nothing to be afraid of. *Yet.* All you're doing is requesting more information about the franchise. How badly do you want to be your own boss?

4—Research. Great franchise business research will help you alleviate some or most of your fears. You just need to know how to do it. I'll cut to the chase; the best way to get your questions about the franchise answered (and you'll have a ton of them!) is to call and visit existing franchisees.

While it's true that most of the information you'll be receiving is courtesy of your franchise development representative, the deep, insightful information you'll need to make a fact-based decision on whether to *actually* purchase the franchise will come from franchisees. After all, they're living and breathing the business you want to own. And they've invested their money into the franchise you're interested in buying.

That's it. Follow these steps and you really *can* choose and research a franchise business in a relatively short amount of time.

RESOURCES

The Franchise King: https://www.thefranchiseking.com/the-franchise-king-website-and-blog-start-here

Net worth calculator: https://www.thefranchiseking.com/free-net-worth-calculator-from-the-franchise-king

HACK 9

HOW TO PRICE YOUR PRODUCTS

WHETHER YOU'RE ALREADY in business or just getting started, setting prices for your products is key. The first rule is small businesses should never try to compete on price—it's an impossible task. Here's how to price your products correctly.

1—Calculate your costs. First, determine how much it costs you to make or buy your product. This is called the cost of goods sold (COGS). List all the direct costs related to your product, such as materials or supplies, equipment used and labor. COGS also include costs directly related to selling the goods, such as commissions or salaries for your sales team or the purchase and maintenance of company vehicles they use to make sales calls.

2—Assess your expenses. Add up your general and administrative (G&A) expenses. These are the costs of doing business that are not directly related to making, obtaining, or selling a product. Frequently, you will need to separate your overhead expenses related to COGS from those related to G&A. For instance, if your building includes a warehouse where you store inventory, the rent on that portion of the space would be considered COGS, but the rent on the rest of the offices would fall under G&A expenses.

3—Calculate your gross and net profit. Subtract your per-unit COGS from your product's per-unit selling price and you'll get your gross profit. Dividing gross profit by gross sales will give you your gross profit margin. You pay G&A expenses out of your gross profit, and the money left over is your net profit. Your prices must be high enough to produce enough gross profit to pay your expenses and generate a net profit.

These calculations alone aren't enough to determine your product's prices. You also need to consider other factors including:

» **What do your competitors charge?** The average price your competitors charge is referred to as the market price. However, some of your competitors will charge much less than the market price, while others will charge more. Examine each competitor to assess what factors enable them to charge higher or lower prices than the norm. Do they offer higher quality, better service or added value? Are they sourcing overseas? Can you do the same?

» **Where do you sell?** Depending on the sales channels you use to get your product to market, you may need to adjust your prices. For example, if you manufacture a product, or you sell wholesale to retailers, your prices need to be low enough so retailers can mark up the price and make a profit.

» **What are your customers willing to pay?** Formulas will only take you so far. If your customers aren't willing to pay what you're charging, you'll need to make some adjustments. Whatever you do, don't lower your prices so far that you aren't making a profit.

Remember, prices don't remain static. You'll need to adjust your pricing many times over the life of your small business. The key is when you price it right, you're meeting the needs of your customers and your bottom line.

HACK 10

HOW AND WHY TO INCORPORATE YOUR BUSINESS

DON'T MAKE THE ALL-TOO-COMMON mistake of thinking you don't have to incorporate your small business because you're just "a one-person/home-based/part-time business." If you're running a legitimate business—no matter how small—it needs to be incorporated.

Incorporating your business essentially creates a shield between your business and the personal you. One important reason to incorporate is to protect yourself and your assets from lawsuits.

That's because no matter how small or informal your business is, you could be sued. Suppose your business hits a rough patch and you can't pay a business debt. It's possible the creditor will take you to court to get their money back. Or what if you run a party planning business and a child is injured during a birthday party you planned? Will the parents sue you? If you operate your own accounting company, you could be held liable if you make a big mistake on a client's taxes.

In these and countless other cases, if your business is not incorporated and you are sued, all your personal assets could be at risk—including your savings, possessions, and possibly your family home. And even if the lawsuit is baseless, you still have the legal costs involved in defending yourself in court.

If you are the only person in your business, and you haven't taken steps to determine a legal form for your business, by default you're considered a sole proprietor. If you have formed a general partnership with another person, your personal assets are still not protected.

So how does incorporating protect you? When you incorporate your business, it creates a new legal entity that's separate from its owners. If your corporation owes a debt or if it is sued, the business—not you personally—is liable.

Incorporating has other advantages:

» It makes it easier to separate your business and personal finances, which has tax advantages.

» It helps you establish a credit score for your business so you don't have to rely on your personal credit score.

» If you need to get a loan or look for investors, being incorporated helps.

» Being able to put "Inc." or "LLC" after your business name looks more professional, which can make customers and clients feel more confident doing business with you.

There are several different forms your business can take when incorporating: a C corporation, an S corporation, or an LLC (limited liability company). Here's a quick overview of the differences:

» C corporation: A C corporation pays federal income taxes. However, any dividends paid to the owner (or other shareholders) are also taxed. This is sometimes called "double taxation," and the S corporation form was created to help avoid it.

» S corporation: An S corporation doesn't pay federal income taxes. Any income or financial losses pass through to the owner and get reported on his or her personal tax returns.

» LLC: Limited Liability Companies have a more flexible management structure than C or S corporations, while still protecting your personal assets. Any profits or losses from the business will be reported on your personal tax return.

There are costs associated with incorporating, as well as paperwork you'll need to complete every year. However, when you consider the personal that could arise from not incorporating, the cost is well worth it.

It's best to consult with your accountant or attorney to help determine which form of business is best for you. There are also companies, such as CorpNet, LegalZoom and Incorporate.com that can do much of the work on your behalf. However, when you consider the risk to your personal finances that could arise from not incorporating, the cost is well worth it.

RESOURCES

C-Corp: https://www.corpnet.com/incorporate-c-corporation/?utm_source=Corpnet&utm_medium=Blog&utm_content=8882230311&utm_campaign=Corpnet-Blog

S Corp: https://www.corpnet.com/s-corporation/?utm_source=Corpnet&utm_medium=Blog&utm_content=8882230311&utm_campaign=Corpnet-Blog

LLC: https://www.corpnet.com/form-llc/?utm_source=Corpnet&utm_medium=Blog&utm_content=8882230311&utm_campaign=Corpnet-Blog

CorpNet: http://blog.corpnet.com/

LegalZoom: https://www.legalzoom.com/

Incorporate.com: https://www.incorporate.com/

HACK 11

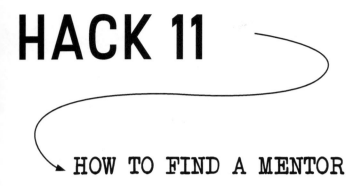

HOW TO FIND A MENTOR

By Bridget Weston Pollack, VP Marketing, SCORE

JUST WHAT IS A MENTOR? For small business owners, mentors are those who are willing to share their knowledge and advice with you—to offer a guiding hand.

And most experts agree: Working with a mentor has a positive impact on small business success. According to a survey by the U.S. Small Business Administration business owners who get at least three hours of mentoring experience increased revenues and business growth.

There are numerous benefits to mentoring:

» Business mentors provide the specific guidance you need. They listen to you and your issues, and provide answers to your questions.

» Helps you avoid timely and costly mistakes by learning from someone who's "been there, done that".

» Increases your level of confidence knowing you have an experienced resource available for simple questions or for more complicated strategy development.

How do you find the right mentor for your business? One way is to put yourself out there, (conferences are a great venue for finding potential mentors) meet people and ask questions. Make your questions as specific as possible, so you're not wasting anyone's time. People are happy to help you, as long as you don't wear out your welcome and respect their time and boundaries.

Mentorship can be a formal, structured relationship, or it can be more informal and unstructured. The key is to find a mentor who is relevant to your business needs.

There is also data—hard numbers—proving mentorship creates greater success for small businesses. A survey of SCORE's clients shows businesses with mentors get a boost starting businesses and creating jobs. Mentored businesses tend to be more successful and stay in business longer.

Mentoring is so effective because it helps you skip past the time and effort of "reinventing the wheel" of business ownership. It helps push an entrepreneur's vision beyond its normal limits. An outside perspective from someone who has been in your shoes can see the footpaths all around— the ones that scale mountains and the ones that avoid treacherous terrain.

One of the best places to find a mentor is at SCORE. At SCORE, we have real-life examples of small business owners who understand the value of a mentor, and how it has helped their businesses.

So, if you're *really* ready to take your idea or business to the next level, don't hesitate to bring in outside expertise today!

Bridget Weston Pollack is the Vice President of Marketing and Communications for SCORE, a national nonprofit that provides free mentoring and education to anyone looking to start or grow a small business.

Resources
SCORE: https://www.score.org/
SCORE success stories: https://www.score.org/success-stories

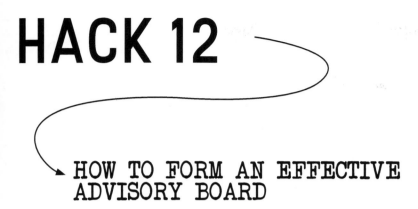

HACK 12

HOW TO FORM AN EFFECTIVE ADVISORY BOARD

IT IS LONELY AT THE TOP. Running your own business can be a very isolating activity with no one to objectively discuss strategy. Many entrepreneurs turn to their lawyer, accountant or a consultant for this type of help, but get little real relief.

A better solution—create an outside advisory board of directors. This is not a legal board elected by the shareholders that comes with fiduciary responsibilities. Rather, this is a board of three to five outside advisors who are selected by you to offer advice, guidance, and direction on key issues.

Here how to create an advisory board:

1—Formulate a strategic plan before setting up the board. If your company does not have a plan about where it is going or what it wants to achieve, then the board will not know the goal with which to measure their actions. Having a plan ensures everyone is headed in the same consistent direction.

2—Find complementary skills. You will need board members who match your organization. This includes not only industry expertise, but marketing, finance, and distribution knowledge. Look for advisory members with skills in areas where you and your team are particularly weak.

3—Build agendas around the three-five biggest issues of the year. Set focused goals on a limited number of topics that can help you *this* year. Being overly ambitious will dilute results.

4—Make sure the board members are prepared. Send out material to the board members at least two weeks before meetings. The quality of the advice the board gives is based on the information they receive. As in so many other things, garbage in, garbage out. This also ensures that not only are the board members prepared, but you are as well!

5—You (or your CEO) must run the meeting. An outside consultant or board member should never lead an advisory meeting. When you run the meeting, you are more likely to get the results you want.

6—Discussion time needs to exceed presentation time. "Data dumps" are not particularly useful to anyone. Limit the time allotted to presentations and the length of any PowerPoints. The focus should be the discussion among the board members.

7—Give access to senior management. Do not hide your management team from the board. A lot can be learned about company dynamics by taking directly to them.

8—Don't be afraid of conflict. It is normal for business groups to shy away from conflict. However, conflict can be vital to a productive discussion and add to the chemistry of the group. The key is to learn how to "fight" nice.

9—Do an assessment of the meeting right after the meeting. Get immediate feedback on how the meeting went. Self-assessment and monitoring is a key to any effective group.

10—Pay your board advisors. Most board members get paid about $1,000 per meeting. Paying this small honorarium will ensure attendance and productivity of the board.

MANAGEMENT HACKS

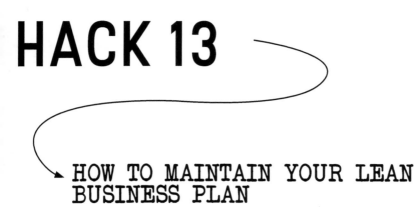

HACK 13

HOW TO MAINTAIN YOUR LEAN BUSINESS PLAN

By Sabrina Parsons, CEO, Palo Alto Software

O NCE YOU HAVE CREATED your Lean Plan (see Hack tk), Lean Management is the process of engaging in, reviewing and comparing the planned numbers with the actual numbers. If you go through the process of creating a forecast, you will be forced to think through things like cost of goods (COGS), Gross Margin, AR and AP days, marketing costs, etc. Once you finish forecasting and you set targets for all these key metrics, you are one step closer to being able to manage your business more efficiently and get better and better at innovating and growing.

The next step in the Lean Planning and Management process is to set up a monthly review meeting. Review your planned numbers against your actual results. Anywhere there is a variance, analyze it. Why were your numbers wrong? What assumptions did you make that are not true? You may have thought you could collect money from your clients every 30 days, but as you review and compare your actual results, you may realize you are actually collecting money every 55 days.

With this information, you can then look at the implications it will have on your cash flow, and do something to prevent any cash problems. You could decide, for instance, to spend more time and effort collecting money to shorten the collection gap. Or you could decide to talk to your banker and get a line of credit, to float you over the longer AR period. Either way, by planning and actively managing to that plan, you have information you may not have previously had. You can directly see the impact of longer collections days on your cash in your bank account.

The last step in the Lean Planning and Management process is to make small adjustments to your plan, preferably no more than once a quarter, based on the variance between your plan and your actual results. The process of comparing these two numbers and understanding why the reality is different than the plan will allow you to see what decisions can actually change your financial picture, and how you can truly grow your company. This is similar to the Lean Startup idea, in that you need to throw ideas and technology out to customers, gather data, then tweak and relaunch. In this scenario, you make educated guesses about what you can do, then you see what actually happens, then you tweak your plans and see what happens. Rinse and repeat.

Once you are actively managing your business using this lean innovative process, you will find it easier to set goals and financial targets, and then taking the time to measure these goals and targets, get data about them, and then adjust when necessary. Lean management makes launching new products and services less "risky." You can target a minimum viable product or service, set some financial goals for it, launch it, measure it, and then tweak what needs to be tweaked based on the results. If you are spending more money than planned to deliver a service, for instance, you can go back and see where you can tweak your service to make the margins you need. Do you need raise your prices? (See Hack TK) Are there ways you can implement the service that are more cost effective?

As you get more comfortable with Lean Planning and Management, you may also want to think about some other metrics to forecast, and then measure against actual results. If you run an e-commerce site you may want to forecast and track unique visitors per month, and an e-commerce conversion rate (ECR). If you run a restaurant you may want to track not just revenue per month, but table turns per week, or per month. If you run a service business you may want to track new clients vs. retained clients.

You need to think through some of the other important key performance indicators (KPIs) for your business and make sure you are including them when you create your Lean plan, and then using the forecasts to help you understand the actual results.

Lean Planning and Management makes innovating and adding new or different products and services to your mix less risky. You have a process in place to make plans, the ability to measure your results against those plans and make calculated adjustments. There is no better way to manage a business for a small business owner.

Knowing exactly where your business is financially, compared to a plan you have put together, lets you understand whether there are problems or solutions to problems long before they actually affect your business. Without a process like this, as the CEO of a business, I know I would have more stress, more sleepless nights and potentially an ulcer. Using Lean Planning and Management I know where my company is headed, and whether I am actually driving in the right direction. Every day, every week, every month I can make small adjustments, and make sure I continue to head in the right direction—UP!

Sabrina Parsons is CEO of Palo Alto Software, developer of the best-selling business management software, LivePlan. A graduate of Princeton University, Sabrina assumed the CEO role in May 2007 and is responsible for Palo Alto's business planning, fiscal and strategic goals and all of the company's traditional marketing.

RESOURCES
Palo Alto: http://www.paloalto.com/
Lean Business Planning: http://leanplan.com/

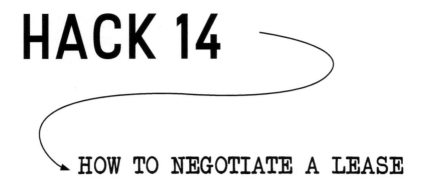

HACK 14

HOW TO NEGOTIATE A LEASE

By Zane Smith, Attorney, Zane Smith & Associates

HERE ARE FIVE CONSIDERATIONS for small businesses looking to negotiate a commercial lease. This hack is limited to an office-type lease; retail leases have significantly different rules and regulations.

1—Decide whether or not to use a broker. The first decision that a business owner must make is whether to find a space with or without the use of a broker. In commercial leasing, there are two kinds of brokers: those who represent the landlord and those who represent the tenant. Usually the tenant brokerage is the most advantageous to the business owner, however the business owner should keep in mind that the landlord is going to try to recoup the cost of a brokerage commission in the lease itself, which is usually one month's rent for every year lease. Once a business decides whether to use a broker or deal directly with landlord, the negotiations begin.

2—Determine what's included in your rent. Commercial leases are different than residential leases in that commercial leases can be net, double net or triple net. In a net lease, the tenant pays the monthly rent plus their own their own utilities. Double net usually means the tenant pays their rent, utilities, share of the taxes and Common Area Maintenance (CAM). Triple Net usually means the tenant pays all those costs, plus the costs associated with maintaining the building, including but not limited to, the costs of the mechanicals (HVAC, fire suppression, roof, etc.) maintenance and repair. A triple net lease is like owning the building without actually taking title in terms of costs.

It is very important for a business owner to understand that the cost of their monthly rent is usually just the beginning of the monthly expense that will be needed to occupy the space. In addition to base rent, utilities, and CAM's, commercial leases usually provide for annual increases in rent as well as cost of living or inflationary increases. Small business owners looking to lease in a newly constructed building should also be aware that building taxes may be artificially low at first due to local government incentives for redevelopment disappearing over time.

It's imperative that a business owner know what to expect, not only in the beginning of the lease term, but also as the lease progresses, so they can budget accordingly.

3—Demand Concessions. In negotiating the lease, you can demand concessions in order to commit. These can include rent abatements (free rent) for up to one month for every year of the lease, buildout concessions where the landlord will pay the cost of rehabbing the space to suit your needs, or rent concessions in the form of less rent at beginning of the lease and more rent at the end. These negotiations are all based on the landlord's expectation that they will recoup these expenses over the term of the lease. The longer the term of the lease, the more generous the concessions usually are.

4—Negotiate an early termination clause. It is possible that the business environment changes and the business owner needs to terminate the lease. In this case, there are terms that need to be negotiated at beginning of the lease, not after it has already been signed. It's not uncommon to have a five-year lease with a negotiated termination agreement after two years. At the same time, the lease negotiation should include any options to extend the lease, such that at end of a five-year lease, if the business wants to extend for another five years, the terms are already negotiated for a set price.

5—Hire an attorney. The terms and price of terminating the lease should be negotiated at the beginning if at all possible. If not practical, the best way to handle a lease termination is to hire a lawyer. Lawyers are usually very successful in calling landlords and telling them that their client's financial condition has changed, or that their client has been bought out, and we'd like to begin negotiations for termination of the lease. The result very much depends upon the skill of your attorney and their ability to negotiate the best possible terms of a divorce.

In summary, lease negotiations carried out by a commercial broker and experienced real estate attorney will usually result in the terms of a negotiated lease that are acceptable to both the tenant and the landlord.

Zane Smith has been practicing law in Illinois since 1983.

RESOURCES

ZaneSmith.com: *http://zanesmith.com.*

HACK 15

HOW TO SET UP A SHAREHOLDER AGREEMENT

THIS IS A STEP T many new business partners frequently miss. Unfortunately, when they sell the company (or if one partner wants to leave), it becomes a nightmare. Use this hack as a template to make business decisions around your partnership and then find a good lawyer to construct a legal agreement you can both sign.

1—Choose titles. This becomes important even if there are two equal partners. In that case, one should be CEO and the other President. Determine what the roles of each partner will be. For example, one will handle sales, marketing and finance. The other will focus on product development, operations and service.

2—Who is on the board? Will the seats be assigned by shareholder ownership? Will this just include the partners or will there be other shareholders (or outsiders)? Will some board members only have observer status?

3—Stock. Will there be more than one class of stock? How will new stock be issues and sold? Will they have different voting rights? Many times, investors are given preferential treatment.

4—Decision-making. How will decisions be made? Will majority rule in all cases? What happens if there are only two partners and the vote is split? Many times, companies set this provision up that decisions are made by majority except in certain cases like issuing more stock, getting debt, annual budget, selling the company, etc.

» **Who is on the board?** Will the seats be assigned by shareholder ownership? Will this just include the partners or will there be other shareholders (or outsiders)? Will some board members only have observer status?

» **Stock.** Will there be more than one class of stock? How will new stock be issued and sold? Will they have different voting rights? Many times, investors are given preferential treatment and given preferred stock.

» **Decision-making.** How will decisions be made? Will majority rule in all cases? What happens if there are only two partners and the vote is split? Many times companies create a provision stating that decisions are made by a majority vote, except in certain cases, such as issuing more stock, getting debt, annual budget, selling the company.

5—Shareholder exit. Since in a small company, stock transfers are typically restricted, how will shareholders leave the company if they want or are forced out? Examine each situation: Voluntary, force out, disabled, and death. Any additional provision that is added typically is that a shareholder must sell if they get divorced to prevent the spouse from becoming a shareholder.

6—The value of the company. When a shareholder leaves the company, how is the value determined? This can be done through a third party or a predetermined formula like a certificate of agreed to value.

7—Will there be a non-compete? When a partner or active shareholder leaves, will there be a non- compete and what will it include (and for how long)? Try to make this as narrow as possible so it is enforceable in your state.

8—Solving problems. Many agreements include a required arbitration clause for dispute resolutions so disagreements don't immediately go to court.

HACK 16

WHAT TO DO IF YOU GET SUED BY A CUSTOMER, VENDOR OR EMPLOYEE

By Zane Smith, Attorney, Zane Smith & Associates

Unfortunately, most businesses will be a party to a litigation at some point in their career. Here is what you can expect and how to react when it happens.

1—Don't ignore a lawsuit. Congratulations! You've just been served with a summons and now are a defendant in the American legal justice system. Do not panic and do not do nothing. If you are sued, you must take action by either responding to the suit, moving to dismiss the suit, or answering the complaint. Doing nothing is the worst possible position that you could take. For example, if you are sued by a customer who says he was permanently injured while walking through your business and you do nothing, it can result in a default judgment against you for an exorbitant about of money. The plaintiff will request a blank check and court will give it to him.

2—Call your insurance company. The first phone call you make should be to your insurance company. Tell them what happened. If your liability insurance covers the claim the plaintiff is making, that insurance company will pay for your lawyer.

3—Collect documentation. It is amazing how quickly we forget details! Write down all the facts that surround the incident as soon as possible. It is also important to collect any documentation surrounding the potential litigation, including receipts, security camera footage, photos of the incident area, photos of the parties involved, and put it in a file. At some point, you will be asked for all this information and you don't want to be scrambling around looking for it or trying to track down an employee to get them to tell you what happened two years ago.

4—Know the client-attorney privilege. You may have to produce a lot of information to the other side of the litigation, however this does not include any communication you have with your insurance company or lawyer. The communication between you and the attorney is protected by the attorney-client privilege. You should be absolutely truthful with your attorney even if results in bad news, because lying to your own lawyer is never good idea. It's important to give them all the information so they can appropriately defend you.

5—Make a good business decision. In litigation, there is a pleading stage, a discovery stage, and a trial stage. Less than 10% of all litigation goes to the trial stage. In other words, over 90% of cases settle, and for good reason. When cases go to trial, one side wins and one side loses and the result can have far-reaching effects. Many times, clients demand their cases go to trial on principal; They say they will never give the plaintiff any of their own money, even if its money paid by insurance company with no out of pocket expenses. While this is an admirable position, the truth is that the business owner has an obligation to their business, and their shareholders to make the best possible business decision that they can. Personal animosity needs to be left out of the decision-making process. That is not to say every case should be settled and every plaintiff should be paid, but that it is important to make a detached business decision. When emotional cases go to trial, the results are unpredictable. Think carefully about whether to proceed with litigation or resolve it in a way that both sides walk away equally unhappy.

Knowing how to respond to a lawsuit is an unfortunate but necessary part of modern day business. It is the business owner's responsibility to immediately respond to any litigation and act carefully and deliberately through the process of defending the cause of action.

Zane Smith has been practicing law in Illinois since 1983.

RESOURCES

ZaneSmith.com: *http://zanesmith.com.*

HACK 17

HOW TO BE MORE PRODUCTIVE IN LESS TIME

T HE ONE THING THAT SMALL business owners have in common is that their to-do list keeps getting longer as the day gets shorter. This is because most people confuse being busy with being productive.

Being busy is just doing stuff at the office; being productive is specifically working on things that will move the company ahead. To run and grow a profitable business, each owner needs to figure out how to be productive, not just settle for being busy.

Here are actions small business owners can take to be 100% more productive:

1—Choose two tasks. Use five minutes at the end of the day to make a prioritized list of two things that must get accomplished the next day. Do these first before opening up email, checking social media or doing anything else on your long to-do list. Choose these two items by answering the question *"What two tasks, if I completed them today, would make my day productive?"*

2—Turn off notifications. Stop being reactive. Make sure you control the attention your electronic devices want and that they do not control you with nonstop notifications. Turn all these off including your phone for set periods during the day. If you work in an office, put up a sign to prevent interruptions at certain times.

3—Stop multitasking. It is a myth that multitasking helps you to get more done. It actually allows you to partially complete more tasks poorly. The brain can really only focus on a single task well. Instead of completing two things with average proficiency, do one thing "fantastically" well. In this way, having a split focus makes you less productive. I have a sign on my computer that simple says "FOCUS" which has helped me a lot.

4—Track your time. The only way to truly know how you are spending your time is to track it. Use time tracking software on a smartphone or desktop such as Toggl to become aware of your work habits, so you can actively change them. When you see what you are actually doing, you'll be amazed how much of it isn't productive and how many times you switch tasks hourly.

5—Hold 15 minute meetings. Most subjects can be handled in less than 15 minutes. Put all smartphones on the table so no one can use them. Standing during meetings will always shorten them.

6—Get your inbox to zero. Most inboxes are a mess. Do a massive inbox cleaning weekly. Delete messages and organize them into separate folders to get to the goal of having zero unread messages in your inbox. Unsubscribe to unnecessary newsletters you never read. After this massive clean is done, commit to handling every email only once. After reading it, reply, delete, file or set for follow up to get it out of your inbox.

7—Create templates. Most communication is repetitive. Create templates for different types of customers and prospects to prevent from rewriting the same emails over and over again. Use a password manager instead of trying to remember all the different ones that are set.

8—Take a break or get some rest. Take a break about every 90 minutes. Continually monitor yourself and your productivity level.

Getting up from your desk to grab a snack or water can be just what you need cut that hour-long task in half. Experts show the key to being more productive is to get a good night sleep. Try a sleep machine app that plays sounds, making it easier to fall asleep (especially when in a noisy hotel room).

RESOURCES

Toggl: https://www.toggl.com/

Best password managers: https://www.pcmag.com/article2/0,2817,24 07168,00.asp

HACK 18

HOW TO BEST COMMUNICATE WITH YOUR PARTNERS

WORKING WELL WITH your partner is one of the most critical factors in setting your company up for success. It is also one of the most elusive goals to achieve.

The first thing to acknowledge is that business partnerships are similar to marriages, except without the sex (and the in-laws). Therefore, effective communication and preserving trust are two critical skills for all partners to practice by following these simple rules.

1—Schedule regular times to meet either daily or weekly face to face or by video. It's easy for communication to break down if there is not an ongoing effort to have personal and private communication. This can be for as little as 15 minutes. Part of the time should be spent checking on how each other is doing personally, so you feel invested in each other's life.

2—Keep it simple and honest. All communication needs to build a trusting relationship between the partners. Evasive answers or questionable motives will hinder the company's growth.

3—Listen to the other side. Don't be so quick or defensive of your opinion. Trusting a partner means believing that their point of view is valid. Make a final decision that is truly in the best interest of the entire company.

4—Don't be angry for more than 24 hours. Staying angry at each other actually accomplishes very little. Be committed to finding out with your partner what the source of the anger is and working through to resolution. Holding a grudge against them is also counterproductive.

5—Don't air grievances about your partner in front of employees. This accomplishes nothing except for the team to be less supportive of the other partner. This is like getting kids to take sides against one parent or the other or staging a political coup. Any complaints should be directly discussed in private with that partner because that is the only place where there can be resolution.

6—Stop back channel communications from employees to partners. Some team members may work for your partner and then seek your help in convincing that partner to do something for them. Don't be fooled by this backchannel maneuver that could hurt your relationship with your partner. Tell the employee that anything they tell you will be relayed to the other partner.

7—Celebrate together. Many times, partners only work together when there are problems. Make sure that you celebrate the successes with your partner as well at work or off hours.

HACK 19

HOW TO SPY ON COMPETITORS-LEGALLY

"Keep your friends close and your enemies closer."
-Sun-Tzu, Chinese general

K NOWING ABOUT YOUR competition has always been important in the world of business. With the Internet, this marketing intelligence has never been more available, but it does take planning. By doing the right type of research, any company can find where their competitors are strong (so you can copy it) or weak (so you can take advantage of it).

Here is how to do it:

1—Always follow them. Sign up for their company newsletter or mailing list. Like and follow their company pages and their personal executive profiles on Facebook, Twitter and LinkedIn. Create a special group or lists for your competitors on these tools, so it will be easier to identify what they are posting.

2—Mystery shop. The best way to understand what your competitor sells and the customer experience they provide is to actually buy their product or service. An actual buying experience will show how good their communication is with their customers. Analyze what their product looks like when it is delivered. Explore their post-sales support to see if there are things that can be adapted for your company.

3—Ask a question. Do this through the various communication channels like email, Twitter, Facebook, phone (text) and their website. Examine their quickness of response and how complete their knowledge is when answering customer sales or service inquiries.

4—Call with a complaint. How do they respond? Do they follow up to completion or do you need to keep explaining the issues over and over again?

5—Explore ad monitoring tools. Find out where your competitors are advertising and which keywords they are targeting. Tools like AdBeat, AdGooRoo and Moat will help find out what ads and keywords your competitors are using.

6—Find their backlinks. Backlinks are still an important element in organic search engine ranking. Use tools like Moz's Onsite Explorer and Majestic Site Explorer to find the backlinks your competitors have on their sites. There may be an opportunity to link your site to the same backlink or use them for customer referral sources.

7—Track their website traffic. Your competitor's amount and sources of traffic can be an important comparison. Use tools like Alexa or Similarweb to get the information you need.

8—Find out what customers are saying. While, it is critical to find out what customers are talking about on the web, it is equally as important to understand what they are saying about your competitors. Put your competitors' name in tools like Google Alerts and Talkwalker, and you'll get an email anytime a new comment about them gets posted on the web. Social Mention and Topsy can also be used for one-time searches about competitors overall positive or negative sentiment analysis.

9—Determine their social media presence. See how your competitor is doing on Facebook. Use tools like Fan Page Karma to find out their reach. A similar process can be done on Twitter with Follower Wonk.

10—Track their technology. Determine what platform and add ins your competitor uses and where they can be vulnerable. Use Builtwith to find this out.

11—Explore web site content changes. Want to know if when your competitor is changing their website? Use Copernic to track updates or particular keywords.

Remember, assume all information is public these days and whatever spying you are doing on your competitors, they are probably doing the same to you!

Resources
AdBeat: https://www.adbeat.com/
AdGooRoo: http://www.adgooroo.com/
Moat: http://www.moat.com
Moz's Onsite Explorer: http://moz.com/researchtools/ose
Alexa: http://www.Alexa.com
Similarweb: http://www.similarweb.com
Talkwalker: http://www.talkwalker.com
Social Mention: http://www.socialmention.com
Topsy: http://www.topsy.com
Fan Page Karma: http://www.fanpagekarma.com/
Follower Wonk: https://followerwonk.com/
Builtwith: http://builtwith.com/
Copernic: http://www.copernic.com/en/products/tracker/index.html

HACK 20

HOW TO BRAINSTORM INNOVATIVE IDEAS IN YOUR BUSINESS

I T IS HARD TO COME UP with innovative ideas solely on your own. This is why collaboration with your peers and staff are so important. Unfortunately, it usually takes the form of team members being locked in a room for a day, where the walls of the room get covered in easel paper and sticky notes. It always seems the loudest people on the team are having a competition on who can contribute the most ideas, regardless of whether they are good or not. Other peoples' eyes glaze over, or they're using social media or answering emails since the session seems to be going on forever and it has long lost its relevance to them.

Typically group brainstorming methods don't work since the democratization of ideas (everyone contributing equally) usually isn't the ideal way to get the best innovative ideas from any group. This is because team members play "too nice" and just follow the majority's ideas. Loud people shout out their ideas just to be heard. Others are scared to speak their mind, so they become disengaged, "hide" and stop participating. The group looks for a "middle" ground where everyone can agree just to complete the exercise.

Here are group brainstorming hacks that will to lead to better results:

1—Identify the actual problem to be solved now. Far in advance, tell team members the specific problem the session will try to solve. This needs to be very focused and not, for example, "How to increase sales". Instead, the questions could be, "How can we retain the value current customers longer". Make sure everyone understands the details of the problem and what solutions have already been utilized to fix it.

2—Prepare individual ideas ahead of the meeting. Before a scheduled brainstorming session, pose the work problem to the group well in advance and ask them to submit ideas. This ensures that all of the team members contribute their current best thoughts before anything begins. This makes for a better starting point than hearing them during the brainstorming session where they are likely to be edited by that person to fit the group dynamic. These ideas are then displayed individually at the meeting.

3—Use an independent decider. Brainstorming methods are best implemented without a democratic framework. There should be a "decider" outside the company hierarchy so they do not give preference to senior leaders during the process. They will determine who talks next and how the group interacts. Team members should be told about the structured process the brainstorming method will follow so everyone knows what to expect. At the end, the decider can truly pick the most innovative ideas that come out of the session.

4—Encourage criticism. Most brainstorming methods involve the idea that there are "no bad ideas" and everyone should be supportive. Unfortunately, this typically only leads to getting a lot of mediocre thoughts. Instead, have the decider encourage critical evaluation of all ideas. Including why something will work or may not work can spark a better solution.

5—Resist the room. Most brainstorming methods happen in some form of a conference room. Staring at walls may not bring out the innovation in most people. Instead, find creative meeting spaces, such as Catalyst Ranch that can help generate ideas. This is a place where team members can free associate with many of the strange objects that may be in the room. Other spaces might include local botanical gardens or other green places. In addition, have people move where they are sitting in the space every hour so they do not get too comfortable and see the conversation from different perspectives.

6—Use tricks to spark critical thinking. Ask the group how to achieve the opposite of what the company actually wants to do. For example, "how can we lose customers as quickly as we gain them?" Not only is this fun, but it is then easier to get people to flip to talk about the best ways to keep customers. Adding unrealistic constraints can also get team members thinking critically. For example, tell them the budget to solve the problem is only $100 and see what they come up with.

After any brainstorming session, only a few ideas should be worked at a time. Ensure there are follow ups to these which include who is assigned to the tasks and when they are to be completed. Determine when these results will then get integrated into the company's daily processes so they become reality.

RESOURCE

Catalyst Ranch: http://www.catalystranch.com/

HACK 21

HOW TO BECOME AN INDUSTRY EXPERT

IN TODAY'S WORLD OF social media, your business success is often tied to your public persona and personal image. One way to stand out in a crowded field, enhance your image and boost your business all at the same time to become known as an industry expert. No matter what your industry, your reputation matters. Want to establish your expert bona fides? Try these ideas.

1—Select a niche. Focusing on one specialized aspect of your industry that's related to your business specialization will increase your chance of becoming an expert. When you hone in on a smaller niche, it's easier to learn everything there is to know about it and find the right audience.

2—Raise your profile. You should already be regularly participating at industry events, such as trade shows and conferences. And you should be a member of your industry association. However, to take your visibility up a notch and be perceived as an expert, increase your involvement. Don't just attend an industry event as a guest, help organize it, offer to be part of or moderate a panel, teach a workshop or give a keynote. The more often you speak in front of groups about your area of expertise, the more respected you'll become as an expert.

3—Promote your expertise in your marketing. If you have an email newsletter, each edition should include an article, blog post or opinion piece you've written on the topic that you want to establish your expertise. Add a blog to your business website with blog posts, infographics and videos sharing your industry knowledge. (See Hack XX). Interview other people in your industry to include in your posts or videos.

4—Share your knowledge on social media. You can expand your influence as an expert even more by blogging for industry websites. You might need to start out by posting comments on relevant blogs. For B2B business owners, LinkedIn is an ideal place to promote your expertise. You can publish your own articles on the LinkedIn platform or simply share useful articles about your industry. Join a few LinkedIn industry groups and answer questions that other group members ask. Don't be too pushy or promotional—the idea is to sell yourself, not your product or service.

5—Use public relations. You can enhance your credibility and reputation by being quoted in industry publications and websites. Develop a list of the media that covers your industry. Follow them on social media (most media people are active on Twitter). Comment on what they're reporting about. It's important to position yourself as a reliable expert source they can contact for commentary, statistics or news about industry trends.

6—Get active in the community. If your business draws customers from your local community, you'll also want to raise your profile in your area, to build awareness. Volunteer to talk to your local chamber of commerce or teach a class at the community college. Look for community organizations that your target customers belong to and think of ways you could offer useful information to them.

HACK 22

HOW TO KNOW WHEN IT'S TIME TO CLOSE YOUR COMPANY

Winners never quit and quitters never win!

Famed football coach Vince Lombardi made this quote famous about when to quit. However, when it comes to small business, this simply is not true. It does not actually help achieve long term success. A better quote that teaches us a similar lesson comes from cowboy Will Rogers:

"When you find yourself in a hole, the first thing you need to do is stop digging".

For many small business owners, the right decision is to close down their businesses and start something else. I value hard work, but having the blind commitment to drive on, no matter what the circumstances are, is not a trait that will always mean success.

Two simple factors should determine whether an owner should quit:

1. **Passion.** Do they still have the passion to continue in their business? Do they still look forward to going to work each day? Lose this drive on a daily basis and it's time to quit.

2. **Cash flow.** Is cash flow steady or is it shrinking? Is there enough cash in the bank to keep going and get through the current stage or is the company running out? Does a capital infusion need to be made from the owner or borrowed from the bank? Negative cash flow means a decision whether to keep going needs to be made soon. Without cash, time is not on the business owner's side.

A lack of either passion or cash flow means it may be the right time to quit. Quitting is not a surrender and it does not mean that you are a failure. Remember that the winners in this world, actually know when to stop. By quitting, the small business owner can stop doing what is not successful and start along a path that changes their trajectory.

The best advice is when you fail, mourn the loss. Have a pity party for 24 hours if needed. Then let go of that failure, and make a new decision that gives you another chance at succeeding.

HACK 23

HOW TO BOOST THE VALUE OF YOUR BUSINESS

By Luba Kagan, Strategic Partners Manager, BizBuySell

THE DAY MAY SOON arrive when you're ready to sell your business. You may even have a price in mind, based on similar businesses that have sold recently in your area. Yet many business owners, after taking a closer look at their businesses in its current condition, are disappointed when they find out its true market value. That's why it's so important to plan ahead now and prepare your business for sale—before putting it on the market in the future.

Here are seven important steps you can take now to boost the value of your business and sell it for a maximum return when you're ready:

1—Increase your profitability. Potential investors will need proof your business is currently profitable. If you can show them these profits will continue to trend upward, you can fetch a higher price. Finding opportunities to reduce costs and create efficiencies leading up to a sale will demonstrate an extra profit boost and impress buyers.

2—Create streams of recurring revenue. Find ways to increase sales and revenue, especially recurring revenue, that will generate income for the new owner—right from the 'get go'. This may include shoring up any pending customer or vendor contracts, giving the new business owner peace of mind they will have consistent revenue flow as they get accustomed to running their new business.

3—Establish processes. Instituting and documenting regimented processes, which enable the company to function effectively without your involvement, will make buyers feel at ease. Potential investors need to be convinced that long after you've made your exit, the business will continue to thrive and run smoothly.

4—Cultivate a high-quality workforce. New owners don't want to deal with employee turnover, especially when they're new to the business. Experienced workers bring balance and stability and help to generate profit. You can increase your company's worth by actively cultivating a high-quality workforce.

5—Stand out and differentiate your products or services. Businesses with differentiated products and services are uniquely positioned to dominate a part of the market. They have an advantage over their competitors and therefore, can command a higher price. You can do this by developing and promoting any intellectual property, patents or other unique feature of your products or services.

6—Identify and highlight tangible and intangible assets. It is essential to list and price all physical assets of your business, including furnishings, fixtures, equipment and inventory. But also consider the value of your intangible assets—things like contracts and agreements, customer relationships, brand recognition, and more. Every non-material asset that contributes to your company's profit line has the potential to boost its price.

7—Mitigate your risks. Put yourself in the buyer's shoes. Do whatever is possible to enhance your company's value. Are your financial records accurate and up to date? Is your facility looking its best? Are there any loose ends that you need to tie up before you list your business? Buyers prefer businesses that come with low risks and high rewards.

Taking these key steps will not only enhance your company's value, it will also grow its sales, improve its profit margins and help it stand out from its competitors. When it comes time to sell, your business will be more attractive to buyers and command a higher price.

Luba Kagan is Strategic Partners Manager at BizBuySell, the largest and most active businesses for sale marketplace.

RESOURCE

BizBuySell: http://www.bizbuysell.com/

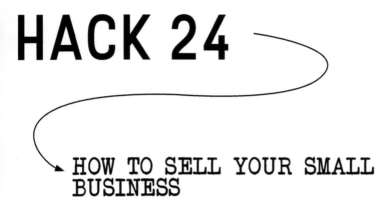

HACK 24

HOW TO SELL YOUR SMALL BUSINESS

BY LUBA KAGAN, STRATEGIC PARTNERS MANAGER, BIZBUYSELL

MANY SMALL BUSINESS owners do not realize selling their businesses may be an option. They may assume if they're not the ones 'opening and closing the door of the business' every day, the business does not have any value. That is likely not to be true. A strategic buyer may value your customer list or your distribution partners or your market niche. Selling your business is an option for many business owners and the more time you take to properly assess, prepare and market your business for sale the higher the probability of maximizing the success of the transaction. Below is an outline of the process and how/what/why/where/when you can expect.

1—Deciding to sell your business. Why are you selling your business is probably the most fundamental question you need to answer—and not just for yourself. This will be one of the first questions a buyer will ask to assess if the business is worthy. There are many different reasons for selling a company and defining the sale motivations and preferred outcomes is probably the most essential part of the process. You should not only define why you are selling the business, but also how you would define a successful outcome. You also need to make sure you are clear on what are you going to do with the money and your time post sale. It is smart to assemble a team of advisors when you are contemplating a sale: these may be your business partners, your life partner, your spiritual advisor, the professionals (accountant, lawyer, business transaction advisor), etc.

2—Preparing for your sale. Get your documents in order. In many cases, small businesses are run to minimize taxes and not to show profit. Realize, when a buyer is evaluating the price/value of your business they likely will use standard industry methods such as multiple of earnings, multiple of sales as one of the ways to arrive at a purchase price. If your sale is several years away (three to five years from now), you may want to start reporting your earnings with this in mind. Yes, you may have to pay more taxes, but if your business is getting bought at 2-3x earnings, your 'tax savings' may be an expensive price to pay. Rule of thumb: Small businesses in general price at .5x sales and 2-3x earnings. You will need some specific documents during the sale process, including:

» Non-disclosure confidentiality agreement
» Personal financial statement form for buyer to complete
» Offer-to-purchase agreement
» Note for seller financing
» Financial statements for the current and past 2-3 years
» Statement of seller's discretionary earnings or cash flow
» Financial ratios and trends
» Accounts payable and accounts receivables aging reports
» Inventory list with value detail
» List of fixtures, furnishings and equipment with value detail
» Asset depreciation schedule from tax return
» Supplier and distributors contacts
» Client list and major client contracts
» Staffing list with hire dates and salaries; employment agreements
» Organization chart
» Photos of business
» List of opportunities for improvement with revenue/profit projections for each

- » Business formation documents
- » Corporate or schedule c tax returns for past 2-3 years
- » Building or office lease
- » Equipment leases and maintenance agreements
- » Business licenses, certifications and registrations
- » Professional certificates
- » Insurance policies
- » Copies providing ownership of patents, trademarks and other intellectual property
- » Outstanding loan agreements
- » Description of liens
- » Products/service descriptions and price lists
- » Business plan
- » Marketing plan and samples of marketing materials
- » Employment policy manual
- » Business procedures manual
- » Other documents unique to your business

3—Determining your sales price. Keep this in mind when you are considering your price and negotiating the offer: Price is important to the seller; terms and conditions are important to the buyer. You may be able to get the highest price you want, if you provide terms and conditions viable for the buyer, be it in seller financing option, transition timing, etc.

4—Due diligence & closing the sale.

Step 1: Prepare for Closing Day: Pre-closing day checklist

- » Schedule your closing when all parties are available. Mornings are preferable since it's easier to reach banks and government officials. Aim for the last day of the quarter, month or pay period to simplify proportion of monthly expenses that transfer with the sale.

- » Finalize the purchase price to reflect the outcome of price negotiation; prorated rent, utility, fees, final inventory value, account receivables, account payables value.

- » Prepare corporate documents. If your business is structured as a corporation, work with your attorney to pass a corporate resolution authorizing the sale.

- » Prepare government and tax forms, including those required by your Secretary of State

- » Confirm insurance requirements

- » Prepare furniture and equipment sale list

- » Prepare to transfer contracts and agreements

- » List and prepare to transfer work in process

- » Finalize list of accounts receivables and accounts payable

- » Prepare loan documentation

- » Prepare to transfer building lease

- » Prepare personal agreements

- » Prepare exceptions to warranties and representations

- » Prepare succession agreements

- » Prepare the bill of sale

- » Prepare the closing or settlement sheet

- » Prepare the purchase and sale agreement

- » Other: based on input from your sale advisors

Step 2: Schedule the Closing. Will your sale close in an escrow office or in an attorney's office?

Step 3: Prepare and review the Purchase and Sale Agreement.

Step 4: Finalize the Deal. For more detailed information on precise steps leading to and at the closing, please check out *How to Sell a Business* session with free resources and books on the process at BizBuySell.com.

Remember the process of selling a business and getting the deal done in the most optimal way for all parties may require a professional, such as a business intermediary/business broker whose forte is in selling small businesses. Organizations such as International Business Brokers Association (ibba.org) is a great resource. Your local business brokers organization may be another. You can also find a list of business brokers on a directory, such as the one on BizBuySell.com.

Luba Kagan is Strategic Partners Manager at BizBuySell, the largest and most active businesses for sale marketplace.

RESOURCES

BizBuySell: http://www.bizbuysell.com/

Guide to Selling Your Small Business: http://www.bizbuysell.com/seller/guide/selling-a-business/

List of business brokers: http://www.bizbuysell.com/business-brokers/

TECHNOLOGY HACKS

HACK 25

HOW TO PICK A NAME (AND DOMAIN) FOR YOUR NEW BUSINESS

C HOOSING A NAME for your business can be easy—or complex. But it's a vital step and can be a determining factor in your future success. Today, when word-of-mouth, internet searches, and social media are all key to marketing success, a business name that's hard to say or spell, or unclear about what your company does, can doom your business from the start.

Before you choose your business name you must be clear about what your business will do, who your customers will be, and what image you're trying to create. Once you understand that, try brainstorming different possible names. Don't name your business after yourself (unless you're a celebrity)—it doesn't convey what you do and makes your business harder to sell in the future.

Think about your long-term goals as well. If you live on the coast and open a pizza parlor called Beachside Pizza, you're limiting your expansion possibilities to other coastal areas.

Before you get too attached to a name, do a quick online search online to find out if the URL is registered to anyone else. Once you've brainstormed about 10 names. Review them and assess whether they're easy to say and spell, how it would look on a sign or website, whether it could possibly have any negative connotations, and how it compares to your competitors' names. What perceptions does this name evoke? Does it say you're serious or fun? This should narrow your choices. Once you've compiled your short list, the Small Business Administration recommends you:

1—Check for Trademarks. Use the U.S. Patent and Trademark Office's (USPTO) trademark search tool to see if a similar name, or variations of it, is trademarked.

2—Check state filing offices. If you intend to incorporate your business, contact your state filing office to check whether the possible name already been claimed or is being used. If you find a business operating under your proposed name, you may still be able to use it, *if* your business and the existing business offer different goods/services or are located in different regions. Consult with an attorney to make sure you don't violate the law.

3—Register your domain name. To claim a website address or URL, your business name needs to be unique and available. After you've searched the web to see if anyone is already using that name, check whether a domain name (or web address) is available. Use the WHOIS database of domain names. If the name you want is available, be sure to claim it right away.

4—Claim Your Social Media Identity. It's a good idea to claim your social media name early in the naming process—even if you are not sure which social platforms you're going to use. Create a social account on all the relevant platforms, so no one else can claim it.

5—Register Your New Business Name. If you are naming your business something other than your personal name or the legal name of your partnership or corporation, you'll need to register as a "Doing Business As (DBA) name or trade name. (This process doesn't provide trademark protection.) Registering a "Doing Business As" name informs your state government you are doing business as a name other than your personal name or the legal name of your partnership or corporation.

6—Apply for Trademark Protection. A trademark protects words, names, symbols, and logos that distinguish goods and services. Your name is one of your most valuable business assets, so it's worth protecting. This is not an expensive process.

RESOURCES

SBA guide to choosing your business name: https://www.sba.gov/business-guide/launch/choose-your-business-name-register

USPTO trademark search tool: http://tess2.uspto.gov/bin/gate.exe?f=tess&state=4804:a6o54z.1.1

WHOIS: https://www.networksolutions.com/whois/index-res.jsp?bookmarked=e01a4eebf2d99a43c66c1032063c.043)

SBA guide to registering a domain name: https://www.sba.gov/business-guide/launch/register-your-business-federal-state-agency

HACK 26

HOW TO GET THE PERFECT DOMAIN NAME EVEN IF IT'S ALREADY TAKEN

By Chris Yates, Cofounder, Rhodium Weekend

Y OU JUST SPENT WEEKS picking the perfect name for your new business. Now it's time to register "perfectname.com," but, when you try to, all you see is the message "Sorry, perfectname.com is taken." Huge bummer. Do you give up? Not so fast! You may still have a shot. Here's how to determine if perfectname.com could still be available and the exact strategies to acquiring it.

LIFECYCLE OF A DOMAIN

It's essential to first understand the different states a domain can be in to determine if you have a shot at acquiring it.

Phase 1: Available. The first state is when a domain is freely available for registration at companies, such as Network Solutions, GoDaddy, or Verisign.

Phase 2: Registered. This is when a person, called the *registrant*, pays to register a domain in their name. A domain can be registered for a period of 1 to 10 years and renewed any time along the way.

Phase 3: Expired. Next, if the registrant decides not to renew their domain by the expiration date, the domain is considered expired. A tool like DomainTools.com can alert you by email if your target domain changes from registered to expired.

Phase 4: Grace Period. The current owner still has the ability to reclaim the domain for the normal renewal cost during an approximately 1 to 45-day window of time.

Phase 5: Redemption Period. In this 30-day stage, the domain can still be renewed by the original registrant but they often have to pay extra to do so.

Phase 6: Pending Delete. This is a five-day hold with the registrar where the domain is locked. You'll want to research ahead of time how a given registrar who holds the domain you want handles what happens next.

Phase 7: Auction. Commonly, valuable domains will then go to auction. In some cases, the registrar runs its own auction. In other cases, registrars partner with auction houses like Namejet.com to run their auctions.

Phase 8: Deleted. In rare circumstances, the registrar may simply delete, also called *drop*, the domain. This means the domain is available to be registered by the first person after the drop. Services like Pool.com can help you catch dropped domains.

Plan of attack to acquire a domain

1. **Researching a domain.** Start by simply visiting the site in your web browser. If you see one or more of the signs below, you may still have a shot at acquiring the domain.

   » Nothing loads or it redirects.

   » An old, outdated, under construction website.

   » A simple or personal website such as a blog.

   » A page with only ads.

   » A page with a link mentioning the domain is for sale.

The next step is to check the WHOIS record (see Hack 26). This record shows the publicly available information about the owner.

2. **Prepare to Purchase.** The next step is to decide what you're willing to pay. One tool you can use to get a really rough value of a domain is Estibot.com. However, a domain is worth what someone is willing to pay for it.

3. **Bid on the domain.** There are typically only a few ways domains change ownership. They include Direct Negotiation, Make Offer, Buy Now, Auction, and Dropped. Bidding through Direct Negotiation, Make Offer, and Buy Now are similar to any other negotiation like buying a home.

   Domain auctions happen in a similar way as an eBay auction. The seller sets a reserve, bidders enter their bids and the auction ends with the highest bidder as the owner of the domain.

4. **Safely transfer.** Speak to an attorney, then go to Escrow.com for the transfer. Money will be deposited, the domain will be transferred to you, and you'll release funds to the seller.

You may need to settle temporarily for a non-ideal domain to get your project off the ground, but if you're persistent there are many ways for you to get the perfect domain even if it's already registered. Of course, once you get the perfect domain, don't forget to keep it renewed so someone else doesn't grab it out from under you.

Chris Yates is a digital entrepreneur who co-founded an exclusive event for entrepreneurs called Rhodium Weekend. He actively buys and invests in online businesses and has advised others in acquiring over $50 Million in established websites safely through his company Centurica.com.

RESOURCES

Centurica.com: http://centurica.com/

Network Solutions: https://www.networksolutions.com

GoDaddy: https://www.godaddy.com

Verisign: https://www.verisign.com

HACK 27

HOW TO SET UP A PROFESSIONAL EMAIL ADDRESS

I F YOU OWN A BUSINESS and send emails on behalf of that business, you need a professional email address. That means you need one that is @ your company's name or @ your name (this especially works if you're a consultant). You should not use a free email account like those from Gmail, Yahoo, AOL or other generic email for your business—it makes you look less than professional. Many surveys have shown consumers believe company-branded emails are more credible.

Although it may initially seem insignificant, there is a bigger takeaway here than just email. It's really all about building credibility and branding; essentially, the impression your business is promoting to the outside world. And for small companies in today's competitive market, branding is how one business will stand out from another.

According to Verisign, there are five reasons why you need a professional, business-branded email address:

1. **Create the right first impression.** While a generic email may raise doubts about whether you're a legitimate business, using a branded email projects a sense of permanence, professionalism and trustworthiness.

2. **Create a "bigger" image.** When people see your generic email address, they may think your business is too new or tiny to do business with. A branded email appears more "corporate". If you have

employees—or even interns—you'll want them to have a professional email address.

3. **Build credibility and trust.** Almost every one of us knows someone who was scammed. Branded emails offer a sense of security to potential customers that you're on the up and up.

4. **It's inexpensive and easy.** You can get a professional email address from a domain name provider or webhosting company. If you're a Microsoft Office 365 user, you can set this up through the Office 365 admin center.

5. **Promote brand awareness.** As Verisign says, "The best benefit of using branded email is every time you send out an email, you're promoting your business. It's a valuable, cost-efficient way to market your company without having to spend a lot of money."

RESOURCES

How to leverage email marketing: https://www.verisign.com/en_US/website-presence/online-marketing/email-marketing/index.xhtml

How webhosting works: https://www.verisign.com/assets/Infographic-WhatIsWebHosting-Sept2015.pdf

Office 365 professional email: https://products.office.com/en-us/business/office-365-business-email-and-shared-calendar-services

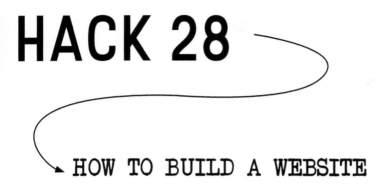

HACK 28

HOW TO BUILD A WEBSITE

A LL BUSINESSES NEED a professional-looking website. This is not debatable—consumers expect all businesses to have a website—and they expect it to be easy to navigate.

Your website does not need to be complicated. At minimum, it should have a home page; a page containing contact information; directions to your business, if you have a brick-and-mortar store; and an About page telling who and other members of your business are and what your business is about. If you are selling products on an e-commerce site, you'll need to have separate pages showcasing your offerings and shopping cart software. Your phone number and address should be easily accessible to site visitors; this assure shoppers you are a legitimate business and helps optimize your site for the search engines.

Of course, your site should feature your logo and be designed in colors that complement it.

Fonts. If your site is not easy to read, consumers won't "stick". That means your fonts need to be legible. They should also reflect the type of business you have. Law firms, for instance, should use a more serious-looking font, while a fashion boutique can use a funkier font. If you market to consumers over 40—your font size should be large enough to be easily read.

Images. Pictures add interest and increase engagement on your site, so make sure to include them. Don't make them so large, however, that they slow the loading of your website.

If you don't have your own pictures, you can find photos you can use at stock photo websites. Most charge, either per photo, or you can subscribe for a specific term. There are also many places that offer free stock photos.

Navigation Menu. The nav bar is a guide for site users to find what they need on your site. It's most often found at the top of the page—and should be on every page of your site so users can easily navigate between pages—and get back to your homepage in a flash.

You can certainly design your site yourself. There are plenty of companies that offer web builders. Before you do that, make sure you have the knowledge—and time to take the DIY approach. Otherwise, hire a web designer to make sure your site looks—and behaves professionally.

Webhost. You will need an entity to "host" your site, unless you buy your own servers (which is rare for most small businesses). A webhost hosts your site on their servers. You can share a server with others, or get your own. The host is responsible for site maintenance, corrects tech issues you experience and maintains up-to-the minute security.

When looking for a webhost, price should not be your determining factor. Compare the services you'll get from the host before you choose one. Make sure you're going to receive tech support.

RESOURCE

Free stock photos: https://blog.snappa.com/free-stock-photos/

HACK 29

HOW TO MAKE YOUR BUSINESS MOBILE-READY

MANY BUSINESS OWNERS think they're mobile-compliant—simply because they've optimized their websites for mobile viewing. And while that is certainly important—it's just not enough anymore. If you want to grow your business, you must incorporate mobile strategies into your business practices.

Mobile technology has become so important because it's increasingly the most common way consumers go online. A report from *Zenith Mobile Advertising Forecasts* says 75% of internet usage will be via mobile in 2017. And "usage" means consumers actually checking their mobile devices 150 to 200 times a day. Research from Facebook shows 73% of consumers *always* have their phones with them. And according to the *Zenith Media Consumption Forecast*, consumers spend an average of 86 minutes a day using the mobile web—compared to 36 minutes on desktop internet.

Take a look at some specifics.

MOBILE SEARCH

When consumers are looking for something, they usually start their hunt by going to a search engine—and today that search engine is often on a mobile device.

Mobile searches in general are on the rise, while mobile searches for something "near me" are growing by 146% year-over-year, according to

Google. (Already, 88% of all "near me" searches are done on a mobile device. Those mobile searches get results—76% of consumers who search online for something nearby visit a business within a day and 28% of those visits result in a sale.

According to the report, *Realizing the Potential of Mobile Measurement* from Google, Bain & Company and Econsultancy, 69% of smartphone owners first search on mobile devices when they need something. And 76% of local smartphone searches lead to a visit to a related business within one day, with 28% of those searches leading to a purchase.

MOBILE EMAIL

So many small businesses rely on email marketing because it's affordable. And it has great potential reach—Statista reports by 2019 there will be 2.9 billion global email users. In the U.S. alone, it's projected there'll be 244.5 million email users by the end of 2017—reaching 254.7 million by 2020.

The DMA (Data & Marketing Association) reports email marketing has a 122% return-on-investment (ROI) and "outperforms all other channels." And 74% of consumers say they prefer (and welcome) email marketing messages from businesses.

Email marketing today *must* be mobile-friendly. And yet businesses are not keeping pace with consumers who have already embraced mobile email marketing. Statista says reading email is the third most popular smartphone activity—86% of Americans use their mobile devices to check personal e-mail.

A study from *Adestra Consumer Adoption & Usage Study* shows nearly 75% of people delete emails that don't look good on their mobile devices—and yet only a small percentage (17% in 2016) of emails are optimized for mobile viewing. In other words, consumers who want your emails are likely deleting them before they're read because they are not mobile-friendly. No small business can survive with those kinds of numbers.

MOBILE COMMERCE

M-commerce—sales from phones and tablets—is booming. Already about 60% of consumers research potential purchases on smartphones before buying—and 65% use tablets. According to Kahuna, 28% of millennials (a huge market just hitting its peak purchasing power), prefer to shop on their smartphones.

Almost half of shoppers say it's now easier to buy products on mobile devices. But they want businesses to offer more promotions, coupons and discounts for mobile purchasing.

RESOURCES

Zenith mobile advertising forecast: https://www.zenithmedia.com/mobile-forecasts-75-internet-use-will-mobile-2017/

Facebook mobile research: https://www.facebook.com/iq/articles/the-thumb-is-in-charge?ref=wpinsights_rd

Think with Google: Mobile-centric search: https://www.thinkwithgoogle.com/consumer-insights/build-your-mobile-centric-search-strategy/

Think with Google: Near-me searches: https://www.thinkwithgoogle.com/consumer-insights/mobile-search-trends-consumers-to-stores/

Think with Google: *Realizing the Potential of Mobile Measurement*: https://www.thinkwithgoogle.com/marketing-resources/data-measurement/mobile-measurement-potential-drive-growth/?utm_medium=email-d&utm_source=weekly-insight&utm_team=twg-us&utm_campaign=20170313-twg-us-think-letter-weekly-insight-a2-OT-PB-CS&utm_content=Mobile-img&mk

Statista email facts: https://www.statista.com/topics/1446/e-mail-marketing/

Adestra study: http://www.adestra.com/resources/downloadable-reports/consumer-adoption-and-usage-study/

Kahuna report: https://www.kahuna.com/blog/infographic-10-critical-steps-to-improve-your-mobile-commerce-strategy/

HACK 30

HOW TO CLAIM YOUR LOCAL LISTINGS

TOO MANY SMALL BUSINESS owners ignore local search because they don't own a restaurant or retail store. But the truth is, every business with a local presence, such as doctors, dentists, remodelers, accountants, lawyers and more can benefit from local search marketing.

The shift toward local SEO is driven by consumers who go online—often using their smartphones—to search for the product or service they need.

Google says 82% of smartphone owners turn to search engines when looking for local businesses to patronize. And 72% of consumers who did a local search ended up in a store within 5 miles.

To make sure your small business isn't missing out you need to claim a listing for your business on relevant local search directories. Start with the ones everybody knows: Google My Business, Bing Places for Business and Yelp. (Don't make the mistake of thinking Yelp is just for restaurants—it's not.)

But don't stop there. Check out local search directories and see which ones are most relevant to your business. Many industries now boast specific search engines, such as TripAdvisor and Houzz. Taking advantage of the interest in local search, Facebook added Facebook Professional Services, a recommendation service you'll want to be listed in as well.

Don't worry about your budget. Most local search services are free, especially for the basic listings. If you want, you can pay for additional features.

The key is to include all the information prospective customers might be searching for, such as your location, phone number, email address, website, hours of operation, and a detailed description of your business using keywords consumers would likely use when searching. Google advises businesses to use the term, "nearby" since 28% of searches for something "nearby" result in a purchase.

Adding photos boosts your search results. If you have testimonials from happy clients and customers, make sure to include them as well.

It is imperative to make sure your listings are identical in each search engine. For instance, don't use the word "Street" in one place and "St." in another

Your listings need to be monitored to make sure they reflect your current situation. And you should check at least once a day to see if customers have left reviews or comments. Answer any complaint immediately (see Hack #96) and thank those who've left positive reviews.

If this sounds like it's going to be too time-consuming, you can download a form filler add-on, enabling you to fill out each form with a single click. There are also services that let you list and update all your listings in one place. Check out LocalWorks, Web.com and Yext, among others.

RESOURCES

Local search directories: http://www.localseoguide.com/best-local-business-directories-seo/

Facebook professional services: https://www.facebook.com/services/

Firefox form-filler add-on: https://addons.mozilla.org/en-US/firefox/addon/autofill-forms/

HACK 31

HOW TO SETUP AN E-COMMERCE STORE ON YOUR WEBSITE

By David Pitlyuk

'M GOING TO ASSUME you already have a product/s ready to sell online. There are a ton of different ways to setup a store online.

Here's how to do so in the quickest, easiest and most cost-effective manner in my experience.

1—Sign up for Shopify. Shopify is the best and most cost-effective way to build a store without the need for technical expertise. Starting prices are inexpensive and provide everything you will need to get going.

2—Choose a theme. There are a number of great free themes provided by Shopify that allow you to customize the look and feel of your store to meet your needs. If you need something more advanced, take a look at Out of the Sandbox. Once your theme is installed, go into the theme settings and check out all the options to modify and get the look and functionality you want.

3—Set All Store Settings. Go through each and every setting for your store and configure everything to your needs. Shopify has great documentation on everything, if you have any questions. This is where you will set up things like how you will accept payment, what you will charge for shipping, setting up a page for customer service, etc.

4—Setting Up Your Products. Now it's time to load your products into the store! Be sure you have good photography and unique product descriptions. Want those professional pictures with white backgrounds? Use a service like Pixelz to do it for you for just few dollars.

TEST

Once you feel like you have everything ready to go, head to your store and test everything. Use it as if you were a customer. Place some test orders. Check it on all types of devices (Mac vs. PC, Chrome vs. Safari, Mobile vs. Desktop). Once you're happy, it's time to launch!

POST-LAUNCH

Now that you've launched, you can start thinking about adding more functionality. One of the reasons I love Shopify is their extensive apps that can add features to your site or connect your favorite email marketing software. Browse through the app store and discover what can work for you.

You should also start thinking about marketing, including social media, email marketing, and advertising. Create ways to collect email addresses for email marketing. You can also use a tactic called retargeting to advertise to customers who have visited your store on sites like Facebook and Instagram.

David Pitlyuk has been involved with e-commerce, since 2001. Currently, he spends most of his time working on Carbon Fiber Gear, (https:// carbonfibergear.com), an online store specializing in products for your life that are made with carbon fiber material.

RESOURCES

Carbon Fiber Gear: https://carbonfibergear.com/
Shopify: https://www.shopify.com/
Shopify help: https://help.shopify.com/

Out of the Sandbox: https://outofthesandbox.com/

Pixelz: https://www.pixelz.com/

Shopify apps: https://apps.shopify.com/

Web.com: https://www.web.com/websites/ecommerce-website-builder

Wix.com: https://www.wix.com/ecommerce/website

BigCommerce: https://www.bigcommerce.com/features/

HACK 32

HOW TO INTERPRET WEBSITE ANALYTICS

By Shama Hyder, Business Strategist & Entrepreneur

A S A SMALL BUSINESS OWNER, you know when it comes to marketing, the only constant is change. Whether you're trying to stay on top of Google's ever-evolving search algorithm, or working to build a presence on every new social media platform that makes the big time, there's always another tweak to be made, another direction to explore, and another strategy to develop, in order to ensure that your marketing message reaches your target audience.

And that's exactly why it's essential to have a solid understanding of your analytic data.

Your website is your most valuable marketing asset online. If it's doing its job right, it'll consistently draw prospective customers, and then guide them through the sales funnel until they eventually convert. You may be able to get a general idea of how well your site is working simply by looking at your sales. But just as in every other aspect of marketing, constant tweaks and adjustments to your site are vital to fine-tuning your strategy, and those changes have to be based on data in order to be effective.

The world of analytics can seem daunting, but if you focus on just a few key metrics, it doesn't have to be complicated at all. The difference these few metrics can make in the success of your marketing strategy is dramatic. Here's how to get started.

1—Connect your website to Google Analytics. Though there are other tools out there, Google Analytics is by far the most popular. Not only is it free, but it provides a truly in-depth look at how well your website is doing just what you want it to do. It's relatively simple to connect since all you need to do is add a tracking code to each page of your site to keep tabs on visitors as they navigate through.

2—Take a look at your traffic. With your website connected, you'll be able to see how many people have visited your site. You can look for seasonal spikes or valleys in traffic, or check to see how any given event may have affected the number of visitors. For example, ran a marketing campaign in March? You'll be able to see how well it worked. Big snowstorm in January? You'll see its effects in the numbers. Knowing how your traffic is impacted by various factors will allow you to capitalize on (or mitigate the effects of) those types of events in the future.

3—Make note of the sources of your traffic. Interpreting your site's analytics can actually offer insight into other arms of your marketing efforts. Google Analytics allows you to see exactly how your visitors find you, whether that's through a web search, a social media link, an ad, or even just typing your site's URL directly. When you know where most of your customers are coming from, you can pivot your marketing strategy to focus more intensely on those platforms.

4—Check out your visitors' behavior. Once you know how they got there, you'll want to see what your visitors did while they were on your site. Maybe they just visited one page and then left. Perhaps they read a blog post, then visited your "About Us" page, then checked out a few of your products, and finally made a purchase. Knowing which of your pages are most successful at moving customers through the sales funnel allows you to change your other pages to be just as effective.

5—Do something about your bounce rate. The number of visitors who leave your site after viewing only one page gives you your bounce rate and your analytics can help you figure out why they're leaving so soon, and what to do about it. You'll be able to see which pages cause visitors to bounce, and tweak them until they begin to lead customers to spend more time on your site.

6—Create custom goals. Finally, Google Analytics allows you to set certain goals for your site, such as getting visitors to fill out a Contact Us form, sign up for an email newsletter, or purchase a certain product. You then can track those specific conversions within Google Analytics to see how well your site is helping you meet those goals.

Shama Hyder is a visionary business strategist for the digital age, and serves as a trusted media resource. You can reach Shama at ShamaHyder.com.

RESOURCE
ShamaHyder.com: *www.shamahyder.com*

MONEY HACKS

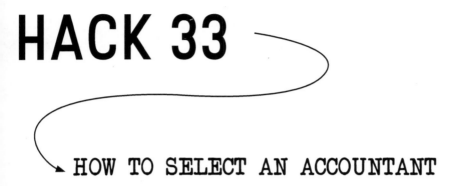

HACK 33

HOW TO SELECT AN ACCOUNTANT

By Jennifer Warawa, EVP of Product Marketing at Sage

BEFORE YOU HIRE AN accountant, ask yourself these seven questions designed to guide you in thinking about what's important to you, so you know you have a winner when you find one.

1. Do you want real-time information on what's going on in your business? The answer is usually yes, but not all accountants operate in real time. Some accountants only send you a PDF copy of your financial statements at the end of the month, and unless you really understand financial statements, this is not the kind of accountant you want. Accountants who work in real-time have access to your data in the cloud and give you information as you need it. For example, if you're deciding between leasing or buying a piece of equipment, they can recommend, based on real-time data, which option is best for your business. Challenge yourself to go beyond financial statements, and start to think about what it looks like to have real-time management of your business.

2. Do you want someone with industry expertise? Most accountants can tell you if your income statement and balance sheet look healthy. When they also understand your industry, they can give you advice that's relevant to you. Evaluate if it's important to you to have an accountant who works with other businesses in your industry.

3. Do you feel comfortable asking questions? An accountant is a trusted advisor who is tied to an extremely personal part of your business, so you want to make sure you have a good relationship. A lot of people talk about meeting with their accountants as if they were getting a root canal. That's terrible! You must feel comfortable asking questions without agony or fear of seeming stupid. Make sure you meet in person or via video chat. A face-to-face conversation, even if it's virtual, is extremely important in making sure you have a good rapport.

4. Who will you be meeting with and how frequently? It's important to understand who your point of contact at the accounting firm is and how they'll be giving you information. Sometimes when accounting firms are trying to get new business, they'll woo you with a conversation with a senior partner, but then you work with the receptionist from then on. Is that okay with you? What if the accountant says the only way they communicate with you is by phone and they'll meet with you once a quarter? Does that work for the way you do business? You might not want phone calls because you're always with clients and text messages work better. Figure out how you prefer to work and whether or not the accountant can work that way.

5. What do references say? You'll want to line up what the accountant is telling you they'll do for you and what they actually do for others. People tend to not bother asking for references because they think it's a waste of time—obviously, they're going to give you a good reference, right? Wrong! I can tell you from interviewing experience that 75% of references picked by the candidates are actually unfavorable. It is absolutely worth having conversations with references.

6. What solutions do they use regularly in their practice? If you have an accounting solution that you love, you want to make sure the accounting firm is familiar with it. Make sure you get a sense of how proficient they are with the software, especially if you're paying by the hour. It can take someone twice as much time to use a software they don't know very well and you're paying for that.

7. How do they bill and when are they available? When accountants bill by the hour, businesses tend to not call for advice. An accountant who embraces value pricing with a set monthly fee is a much better model because business owners are more likely to take advantage of the accountant's services. Finally, evaluate when you need the accounting firm to be available. Is it important for them to be available beyond the typical 9am-5pm work day? You want them to work when it's convenient for you, which may be during your off hours on the evenings and weekends. What's most appropriate for your business?

Use these questions to create a checklist of what you're looking for in an accountant so you know when you have a good match for your business. After all, if you don't know what you're looking for, anyone will do.

Jennifer Warawa serves as EVP of Product Marketing at Sage and prior to working at Sage, had her own accounting, bookkeeping and consulting firm in Kelowna, BC, Canada for 12 years.

RESOURCE

Sage: *www.sage.com*

HACK 34

HOW TO FIND THE RIGHT SMALL BUSINESS BANKER

By Franco Terango, SVP Divisional Executive, Small Business Banking, Bank of America

A GOOD SMALL BUSINESS banker is an expert in lending, but beyond that, they can help advise on financial matters throughout the lifecycle of your business—from simply being a sounding board for your ideas, to helping you develop a solid business plan.

Whether you are seeking your first loan, or are already well-established and looking to work with a small business banker for the first time, here are my top tips to help you find the *right* small business banking relationship to meet your specific needs and goals:

1—Research and explore. When evaluating small business bankers, it can be helpful to research the many options available to you before ultimately deciding who to work with. A helpful tip is to approach it the same way you would in choosing to work with any business partner. To help narrow down your list, ask local business owners, your mentors and extended network for recommendations on banks, or even for specific names of small business bankers they've had a good experience with. Then, make appointments with those banks/bankers on your short list.

If you already have a business banking account, but haven't explored the full extent of the resources your bank or banker offers, set up time for a conversation. If time is an issue (which it usually is!), many small business bankers will meet you at your place of business.

2—Determine your immediate and long-term needs. As you know, securing a loan versus maximizing cash flow are two very different challenges. Before you meet with prospective bankers, determine both your most pressing business needs and how those needs may evolve over time. A good small business banker will actively listen to your concerns, offer recommendations on banking products to best address those needs and provide you solutions. The banker should connect you with resources (above and beyond traditional bank products) where appropriate.

3—Ask questions—a *lot* of questions! As a small business owner, you're not expected to be an expert in finance, so ask away! Some key questions I recommend include:

- » Can you give an overview of the small business solutions you provide?
- » What are the different financing options for my business?
- » How long have you been with the bank?
- » What is your experience within my industry?
- » What is your level of experience working with small and mid-sized businesses?
- » Can you describe your loan process and procedures?
- » What type of paper work will you need from me when securing a loan?
- » What is an estimated timeline for how long it will take to get my loan application in front of the credit committee and, if approved, to loan closing?

4—Demand excellent customer service: This is my tip to help evaluate whether it's time to *switch* banks. Think about recent experiences you've had with small business bankers in person at branches; with customer service representatives over the phone; and with using your bank's online and mobile banking platforms. If those experiences often leave you frustrated, upset or confused, then it's probably time to go back to the drawing board. Repeat steps one to three to find a new bank where you can build a long-term relationship with your banker and have confidence in the customer support and attention you'll receive.

A key consideration for small business owners at any stage of their business: take the time to find the best fit for your business banking relationship. Weighing all the factors, evaluate how well your banker and bank can advise and support you as your business needs evolve. Set clear expectations on how you want to be communicated with (phone, e-mail) and how often. It will, after all, be one of the most important business relationships you have.

Bank of America, N.A. provides informational reading materials for your discussion or review purposes only. Interpretations in this release are not intended, nor implied, to be a substitute for the professional advice received from a qualified accountant, attorney or financial advisor. Neither Bank of America, its affiliates, nor their employees provide legal, accounting and tax advice.

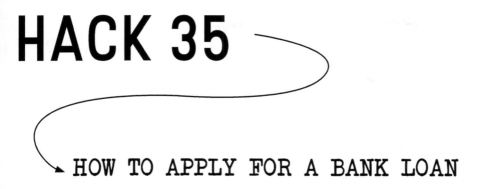

HACK 35

HOW TO APPLY FOR A BANK LOAN

By David Burch, Division Executive, Bank of America

I T'S NO SECRET THAT securing credit is a critical part of owning a small business, but it can sometimes feel daunting. However, with the right combination of planning and research, it really doesn't have to be. Obtaining a loan and finding the right source of credit for your business takes time and effort, and there are several ways to ensure the process goes smoothly.

First things first, when seeking a loan, it's helpful to understand how the lender will evaluate your business. Banks look for the 5 C's when making loan decisions: capacity, capital, collateral, conditions, and character.

THE 5 C'S

1. **Capacity** evaluates whether your business can support debt and expenses. Typically, you need enough cushion to absorb unexpected expenses or a downturn in the economy.

2. **Collateral** includes accounts receivable, inventory, cash, equipment and commercial real estate. Lenders may also take into consideration existing debt that your business may still owe on collateral.

3. **Capital** takes a look at whether your business assets outweigh liabilities; and how much capital you and other outside sources have invested.

4. **Conditions** such as the economy, industry trends and pending legislation may be taken into consideration (these factors are often out of your control, so while you should be aware of them, don't sweat them too much).

5. And finally, **Character**—your own character and the character of those tied closely to the success of your business—is critically important. Factors such as personal integrity, industry experience and good standing can make a difference. Always surround your business with good people.

WHAT DO YOU NEED?

Consulting the 5 C's while preparing to apply for a loan is a key part of the process, and taking the time to figure out what you need from the bank is also helpful. Start by asking yourself what you need the money for, and speak with your banker or a trusted advisor about your options. For example, are you launching a new business, opening a second office, or buying equipment? Loans come in a variety of sizes and payment plans, with subcategories around commercial real estate, equipment and vehicle financing and more. For example, Bank of America offers two main types of small business loans:

» **Business Line of Credit:** A flexible line of credit starting at $10,000, designed for business owners looking for open-ended access to funding for ongoing business needs such as seasonal working capital or inventory management.

» **Business term loan:** A one-time lump sum available for amounts of $25,000 and up, designed for business owners purchasing inventory and equipment or refinancing debt or financing account receivables.

Beyond traditional bank loans, your small business banker can also connect you to excellent opportunities for accessing capital through Community Development Financial Institutions, or CDFIs. CDFIs are private-sector local loan centers that provide affordable credit and financial services to underserved markets and populations. Most importantly, CDFIs encourage and enhance economic growth and development.

Additionally, a small business credit card can help you build credit for your business once it has been established—and a good small business credit history will be critical for when your business is ready to grow. A small business credit card can also help manage your cash flow, because it provides liquidity and can help you separate your business expenses from your personal expenses—which also can help you maintain control over employee spending, and make tax preparations easier.

When selecting a small business credit card, keep in mind some cards have no annual fee, while other cards have a low annual fee with enhanced rewards. Choose the combination that's best for your bottom line.

And don't forget regardless of the type of financing you secure, your small business banker can work with you to help ensure you are taking advantage of bank account cash management, treasury and security services to keep your business running efficiently and safely.

Above all, please don't let the funding process overwhelm you. Remember the 5 C's, talk to your advisors, and take the time to figure out the best option for your needs. At the end of the day, there are many resources at your disposal and people willing to help—all you have to do is ask.

Bank of America, N.A. provides informational reading materials for your discussion or review purposes only. Interpretations in this release are not intended, nor implied, to be a substitute for the professional advice received from a qualified accountant, attorney or financial advisor. Neither Bank of America, its affiliates, nor their employees provide legal, accounting and tax advice.

HACK 36

HOW TO FIND ALTERNATIVE SOURCES OF LENDING

IT CAN BE DIFFICULT FOR A small business owner to get a traditional bank loan. And even if you can, they're often not the best choice for your small business and situation. In many cases, alternative business loans (which are simply loans that don't come from a traditional bank) can be more helpful to you. Here's why:

1—Alternative business loans have shorter term lengths. A traditional small business loan, or *term loan*, generally has a one- to five-year term, which works best if you need the money for a longer time. A term loan from a bank, for example, is a good way to pay for a fixed asset, such as business equipment or commercial real estate.

Alternative business loans, on the other hand, typically have shorter repayment terms—six months to two years, in most cases.

2—Funding is faster. Traditional bank loans typically take longer to get, partly because there's a lengthy application process. First, you have to complete a lot of paperwork; then you wait weeks—or even months—to hear if your loan is approved; and then you have to wait until the money actually gets into your account.

Alternative business loans fund quickly, which is one of their biggest advantages. In many cases, you'll hear back from your lender within 24 hours, and get your loan funded within two days. This is an ideal solution if your business needs cash quickly to take advantage of a business opportunity or get over a short-term cash flow challenge.

3—Less paperwork. It's just a lot easier to apply for alternative business loans, which is a huge advantage. Instead of having to complete a business plan and provide financial statements, tax returns, bank statements and more, the application process is usually a simple matter of answering a few questions online.

4—No collateral needed. To get a traditional bank loan, you often need to put up collateral, which can be risky for your business or your family. In contrast, alternative financing sources almost never ask for collateral.

5—Faster payback. If you take out alternative business loans, such as short-term loans, you will repay the loan faster and get it off your accounts. That's because many of these loans are repaid with daily payments drawn directly from your bank account or business credit card, rather than a monthly lump sum.

You can also delay payback. Traditional term loans require you to start making payments as soon as your loan is funded—even if you don't use the money right away. Depending on the type of alternative business loans you obtain, however, you may not have to pay the money back right away. For example, if you get a business line of credit, you won't need to repay anything until you actually draw from the credit line.

6—Types of alternative lending. The most common forms of alternative lending are term loans, equipment loans, business lines of credit, invoice financing, merchant cash advances and small business startup loans.

RESOURCES

Fundera: https://www.fundera.com

Fundbox: https://fundbox.com

On Deck: https://www.ondeck.com

Balboa Capital: https://www.balboacapital.com

Kabbage: https://www.kabbage.com

Guide to alternative lending: https://www.slideshare.net/Fundera/the-definitive-guide-to-alternative-lending

HACK 37

HOW TO GET MONEY FROM INVESTORS

By Steve Miller, Cofounder & Partner, Origin Ventures

D O YOU WANT TO RAISE capital from outside investors? Here are five things to think about.

1—Assess your needs and make a plan. Before seeking external funding, small business owners must have a plan in place for how much capital is needed and what it is going to accomplish. Ask yourself the following questions: What milestones can be hit with this capital? How long is it going to last? Will there be additional capital needed at a certain point down the road?

2—Understand the ramifications of taking outside investment. Small business owners need to understand what the ramifications are of raising money from outside investors. Often, it means giving up a piece of equity ownership in the company, and that is something entrepreneurs may not want to do. It will also mean that you now have people to report results to, where in many small businesses and sole proprietorships that may not have been the case before. When you take outside investor money, you have a fiduciary responsibility to do what you say you're going to do with the money.

3—Know which type of investor is a good fit for your business.
There are several types of outside investors, including venture capitalists and organized angel groups, as well as friends, family and colleagues. Not all businesses are a good fit for all types of investors.

Venture capitalists and angel investors, in particular, are looking for a substantial return on their investment. To this end, they only invest in businesses that are highly scalable. Venture capitalists invest in companies with the idea that five-seven years down the road, those companies are going to be sold for a value that's 10 times the value at the time the investment is made. The vast majority of small businesses in this country are not appropriate for venture capital funding.

Family, friends, and colleagues in your professional network are likely to be a more appropriate source of investment. These groups most likely won't demand as high a rate of returns beyond their initial investment as venture capitalists or angel investors, and may not require an equity stake in your company. Also playing an increasing role in outside capital is crowdfunding, which on popular sites like Kickstarter and Indiegogo, allow entrepreneurs to connect with complete strangers to raise money for their businesses in exchange for tangible perks, instead of financial returns. Finally, small businesses should consider banks as a source of outside capital. Technically, banks are not investors, but they are in the business of loaning money and do not require dilution of ownership.

4—Pitch yourself! Most investors, no matter what kind, are not going to meet you and say, "You're awesome, here's a check". There must be a pitch involved.

A pitch to an investor is essentially a sales job. It's similar to selling your product and service to your customers, but instead, you're selling a piece of your company to prospective investors. A lot of a pitch has to do with the questions you should have answered when writing your business plan. What does the business plan call for? How long is the money going to last? What milestones is the business going to hit with this money? What is the return on investment? The answers to these questions must be in your pitch.

All investors are investing in the same thing—the people! It's important to sell yourself. Why are you the team they should invest in? Why are you the ones who are going to hit these milestones? What's your background? Do you have a team with proven track record? Are there people who are advising you?

Also, as mentioned above, investors are interested in some sort of return. How is that return going to be structured? Will there be dividends? Will there be a return on capital? This must be spelled out as part of the pitch as well as in the ensuing negotiation.

5—Do your due diligence before taking investor money. It is important to understand what the investors will require of you before taking their money. Have a conversation with them about what their expectations are. How is this relationship going to work? Are you open to advice and counsel, or are you a lone ranger who just wants the money? Both parties need to be comfortable with the arrangement; if the investor is hands-on and the entrepreneur doesn't ever want to hear from the investor, that's going to be a problem. The arrangement needs to be spelled out early in the negotiations.

Ask the investor for references so you can speak with other entrepreneurs in whom they have invested. Ask the entrepreneur what their relationship with the investor looks like. Do they call every five minutes to see how sales are going?

Finally, determine what other value this investor may bring beyond writing a check. Do they bring a network of people they can introduce you to as potential business partners, customers, and/or team members? These introductions are often worth more than the dollars invested.

Steve Miller is co-founder and partner of Origin Ventures.

RESOURCE

Origin Ventures: *www.originventures.com*

HACK 38

HOW TO SET UP A CHART OF ACCOUNTS

THE CHART OF ACCOUNTS is a listing of all financial accounts used in the company. Your accounting software will use the chart of accounts to aggregate information into your business' financial statements. Customizing the chart of accounts for your company is the first step in setting up a financial and bookkeeping system that will keep track of your money. If you are not familiar with this concept, please ask an experienced person to assist you in setting up a chart of accounts.

Here are the items that should be customized for your company:

ON THE BALANCE SHEET

1. **List all cash accounts.** Many businesses have different bank accounts for operating, investing, payroll taxes and merchant accounts.

2. **Are there accounts receivables?** Will customers pay for your product and services when they are delivered or will you bill them to be paid later?

3. **List credit card debt.** Will credit cards be listed under the payable account or as a separate short-term liability?

4. **List long-term liabilities.** List any bank or personal loans the company owes. (Loans are a common source of capital for businesses.)

On the Profit and Loss Statement

1. **Describe what is sold.** Do you want to classify the revenue by different types of what is sold? For example, by product or service type?

2. **Determine costs of service (COS) or cost of goods (COG).** Make sure every direct cost that directly goes into making, buying or shipping your products or services is included to show a clear gross profit.

3. **List payroll.** These costs can go into cost of goods if they are directly attributable in making the product or delivering the service. They can go in general expenses if they are more fixed costs regardless of sales.

4. **All other expenses.** List the general categories of these expenses with enough detail so they can be analyzed. However, too much detail will not allow the owner to look at the big picture. For example, there should be accounts for rent, telephone, insurance, professional fees, marketing, travel, meals, etc., but perhaps not separate accounts for each airplane, train and automobile trip. However, the professional fees should be split between accounting and legal.

A standard chart of accounts is numerically organized. Each major category will begin with a specific number, and then the sub-categories begin with the same number. For example, if assets are classified by numbers starting with 1, then cash accounts might be labeled 1100, accounts receivable might be labeled 1200, and inventory might be labeled 1300.If liabilities accounts are classified by numbers starting with 2, then accounts payable can be labeled 2100 and short-term debt might be listed as 2200.

Most accounting software will have a suggested chart of accounts for your industry.

HACK 39

HOW TO READ YOUR FINANCIAL STATEMENTS

GET OVER YOUR FEAR of the numbers. It's essential every small business owner knows the components of and how to read a financial statement.

A profit and loss statement shows the revenue, expenses, and profit of a business over a period of time. The basic components include:

» **Revenue:** This is a business's sales, resulting from customers buying your products or services.

» **Cost of goods or services (COGS):** This is defined as the direct cost of producing the product or service the business sells; and could be raw materials or labor.

» **Gross profit:** The difference between sales and cost of goods; is also known as the gross margin.

» **General expenses**: Rent, people, insurance, utilities, telephone, travel, etc.

» **Net profit:** This is the difference between gross profit and general expenses. Taxes and depreciation are typically deducted from net profit.

Learn to read a balance sheet. This is the book value of your business at any given point in time. It also measures the ability of a company to pay its debts. Following are the basic components:

Assets: What the company owns. This can include:

» Cash: How much money the company has in the bank

» Accounts receivable: The value and age of the money that is owed the business

» Inventory: The value of the inventory

» Fixed assets: Equipment, computers, and property

Liabilities: What the company owes. This can include:

» Accounts payable: The money the business owes vendors

» Loans: The money the company owes banks and other sources

Owners' Equity: The assets minus the liabilities. This can include:

» Stock: Paid-in capital

» Retained earnings: Profit retained in the company since the start

There are many good resources available to learn how to read financial statements. Get help from your CPA or educate yourself online. Remember, accountants are advisors, not adversaries.

Review your financial statements on a monthly basis. Performing this task will help you gauge the health of your business. Here are three other measurements that help you find important information about your business:

1—The quick ratio (or the acid test) on the balance sheet: This is the business's current amount of assets (cash, cash equivalents, accounts receivables) divided by current liabilities. A favored metric of banks, the quick ratio is a measure of the financial stability of a business. In most industries, the quick ratio should be greater than 1.1. It shows the company has more cash available than current money it owes. When the ratio goes below 11, it means your business may not be able to meet its financial commitments.

2—The business' sales-close ratio in your customer relationship management system (CRM): Of all the proposals your business sends, how many do you win? This is a key number since it should not be too low or too high. If it is too high, either your business is not talking to enough prospects or your prices are too low. If it is too low, you may not be qualifying your prospects enough before preparing proposals for them.

3—Your 10 most important customers: This is not just measured by revenue, but also by referrals, additional products they buy, feedback they give, retention, or their superior brand power.

HACK 40

HOW TO SET AN ANNUAL BUDGET FOR ANY COMPANY

WE ALL LIKE TO SET goals and then strive to achieve them. Yet, why don't more of us make an annual budget for our companies? There are three general hesitations around setting up an annual budget. First, the future is uncertain and it's hard to put numbers to it. Second, if you did put an annual budget down on paper, it may show your company losing money for the year, and that would be depressing. Third, how will you feel and what will you do if during the year, you fail to meet your budget?

Setting up an annual budget of expected revenue and expenses for a company is a critical financial management tool to increase profitability, and ensure there is enough capital to run the company. Here is where to start:

1—Collect all the numbers. Review your annual profit and loss statements from the last two years. Take out one-time revenue and expense bumps that will not be repeated in the current year. Use the information left to calculate the average of these last two years. Adjust the numbers for current year increased expenses, changes in gross margins, market conditions, one-time investments, and projected revenue. It is critical here to review each account category on your annual budget in detail and consider carefully how they relate to each other. For example, will hiring more salespeople result in higher income? Will adding employees increase the company's health insurance expenses? Some fixed costs may not change with revenue (like rent), but others (like sales commissions) will. If this is the first time a budget is being set up, Microsoft Excel has templates you can use.

2—Replace optimism with realism. Annual budgets become ineffective if they are filled with hope, and no realistic chance of meeting those objections. Think through your specific profit goals and why certain numbers are set the way they are. For example, what expense investments are being made this year that will increase sales? If your cost of goods is expected to go down, why? Most small business owners project revenue that's too high and expenses that are too low. When in doubt, cut revenue expectations by 25% and increase expenses by 10%. Ask an accountant or banker to review the budget and raise additional questions you should consider.

3—Add the budget into the financial system. Take this annual budget and divide it by month. It now becomes a profit and loss statement for the upcoming year. Enter it into the company's financial application so each time monthly financial statements are reviewed; they can be compared to this budget.

4—Adjust once a year. Annual budgets can work only if they are utilized correctly. They are a fundamental way to track planned monthly revenues and expenses against actual performance. They answer the question: "How is the company doing compared to what we expected?" Ideally, budgets should only be set once a year, and then changed only every six months. It may make the business owner feel better to adjust the budget to meet their lower performance, but it does not help manage the company. Don't hastily pass judgement on being financially ahead or behind on the budget forecast. Treat any unexpected result as valuable information the company can use to make mid-year adjustments. If after six months, the company is more than 50% ahead or behind the budget, then the annual budget needs to be recalculated, so it can still be a valuable financial management tool.

5—Control and adjust. If the company is not meeting the budget, consider which expenses can be controlled or reallocated. What changes need to be made to hit revenue targets? Asking these type of questions is the exact purpose of the budget. It allows the company to make adjustments that still allow them to meet their goals.

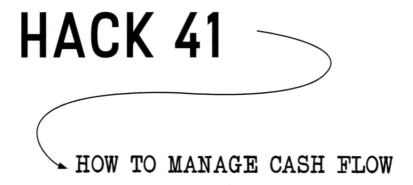

HACK 41

HOW TO MANAGE CASH FLOW

By Robert Okabe, Cofounder & Managing Director, RPX Group

EVERY FAILED COMPANY goes out of business for one reason—they run out of cash. Here are the best hacks to make sure you never do:

1—Use cash-focused financial reports. The accrual method is the accepted form of financial reporting. It matches costs to time periods in a way that allows you to visualize how well your business is functioning. The drawback is the accrual method makes it harder to understand how much money you have.

Most small business accounting software provides an option to create reports using the cash method of accounting which provides a clearer picture of where the money is. For example, the accrual method recognizes a sale when you bill your customer, while the cash method records the sale when the customer pays you. Using cash basis reports regularly gives you the information you need to more aggressively manage cash flow.

2—Manage auto payments. Setting recurring bills for automatic payment can be a great deal—less paperwork, no hassles, a discount for participating. Ever wonder why your vendors offer that discount? To some degree, they are sharing the cost savings, but the hidden value is the benefit of the guaranteed cash flow you provide them by giving up control over when you send them the money. It may be tough to give up the discount, but if your cash flow is really tight, a few days of extra float may be more than worth it.

On the flip side, offering autopay to your own customers can accelerate your cash flow and reduce payment processing and collections costs. Sharing the savings in order to get cash faster may well be a price worth paying.

3—Change merchant processors. If your company takes credit cards, you have a merchant agreement with a payment processing company. Merchant processing contracts make cell phone plans look simple, and you probably dread the thought of revisiting that process. If you haven't reviewed your plan in a while it may be worth the pain. Any reduction in percentage of payments the processor keeps is money in your pocket, and getting that money a day or two faster can relieve day-to-day cash-flow bottlenecks.

Take a careful look at the new breed of merchant processors such as Square and First Data. Not only do they offer lower fees and faster payments, many offer options such as emailing or texting receipts, which gives you valuable customer contact data to use in your marketing.

4—Set up a "Christmas Club". Before the widespread use of credit cards, banks would offer a special type of account often called a "Christmas Club". Customers would make weekly deposits to their Christmas Club accounts and were not allowed to withdraw the money until the holiday season. Turning saving into a routine process helped consumers manage their cash flow and avoid the disruption of holiday spending.

If you need to make a major purchase for your business, consider creating your own version of the Christmas Club account. Beginning about six months before your anticipated purchase date, set aside about two% of the cost of the item into a separate account each week. By saving in advance you'll reduce the hit to your cash flow when you make the big purchase, and saving a small amount each week is much less painful

5—Require customer deposits. If you sell big ticket items or make custom products to order, winning a large order is a blessing—and a curse. You have to buy raw materials and components weeks or months in advance of billing the sale and collecting the revenue. Any caterer that's experienced a called-off wedding knows the pain of cancellation.

Take an idea from the caterer's playbook and require a substantial deposit for unusually large orders. This allows you to use the customer's own money to finance upfront costs and greatly lowers the risk of both cancellation and non-payment. If necessary, offer a one or two% discount in order to secure the deposit. It's cheaper and safer than floating a balance on your credit card.

6—Extending payment terms. You've heard the stories about companies that haven't paid vendors for three, four, even six months before going out of business. Don't be that company or one of those vendors. If one of your customers is experiencing difficulties, make concessions, but be disciplined about them. Make the customer pay something, even if it's only a portion of what's owed. Once their outstanding balance exceeds your limit (two to three months of sales), put them on a cash only basis until their balance falls below your limit.

If your company is having difficulties, pay every vendor something every month. It's a show of good faith and respect for your business partners. Making partial payments buys you time and goes a long way toward gaining concessions.

For the last fifteen years Bob Okabe and his colleagues at RPX Group have helped advance the development of university and corporate innovations through startup companies. You can catch his perspectives on the topic of raising capital for startups at investoriq.org.

RESOURCES

RPX Group: http://www.rpxgroup.com

Investoriq.org: http://www.investoriq.org/

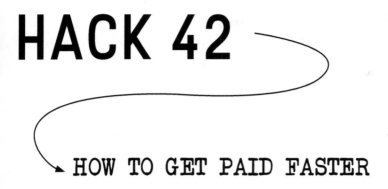

HACK 42

HOW TO GET PAID FASTER

TOO MANY SMALL BUSINESS owners think that in addition to providing whatever product or service they do for customers, they are also a bank for them. This is evident in the way they easily give credit to anyone that buys from them and make little effort to collect their money. In this way, they are actually funding their customers' companies. This is a real problem for any small business since positive cash flow is one of the most important factors to growing a successful company. Unfortunately, not collecting accounts receivables from customers uses important cash that could be used for investments in other parts of the business.

HOW TO COLLECT YOUR RECEIVABLES FASTER.

1—People respect what is asked for. Customers actually respect vendors who want payment and press hard for collections. This is not a sign of weakness, but simply the sign of a small business owner who runs their company well. As in many cases, "the squeaky wheel gets the grease"; these companies are always paid first.

2—Follow a standard process. It is critical to have an internal process in place that starts as soon as an invoice is sent out to the company. Getting the first payment from a client is always the toughest, especially if the business is a large corporation. It is vital to figure out the approval path in matching the invoice to the purchase order, even before the approved invoice gets into the queue for payment. This process should start before the work is even completed. Ask the customer if there is anything that needs to be done to be paid within their system, such as providing a W-9 (tax ID number) tax form. When the first bill is sent, call the company to check if the invoice was received, and ask when it is scheduled to be paid. Right before it is scheduled to be paid, call again to see if the check was sent. If it did not make this "check run," ask when it will be sent. All this can be managed easily with electronic reminders.

3—Go electronic. Check to see if invoices can be paid electronically through direct deposit into the company's bank account. This provides a quicker boost in cash flow by cutting down on mail transit and expediting the bank transfer.

Most companies want to pay their bills. They will, in fact, appreciate these gentle reminders if they are done in a polite and respectful way.

4—Problems. Customers who do not pay are not customers—they are collection problems. It is much better never to do business with a customer who doesn't pay, rather than having to chase them for the payment.

HACK 43

HOW TO MAXIMIZE YOUR PROFIT

By Mike Michalowicz, Entrepreneur & Bestselling Author

KNOW A THING OR TWO about profit. In fact, I wrote the book on it... twice. My book *Profit First* was recently re-released, and as part of my revision process, I reached out to entrepreneurs all over the world who have successfully used my strategies to make their companies profitable. I asked them what really worked in terms of achieving and maintaining profitability. Here's what I learned.

1—Take your profit first. It sounds so simple you may think there's no way it could really work, but it does. Over and over, I hear from small business owners who have finally committed to turning the corner and running a profitable company. Here's how it works: Every single time you bring revenue into your company, you take a predetermined percentage Hoof that revenue and set it aside as your profit. You put this profit in a new account at a separate bank, and you leave it alone (and watch it grow.) You take this profit first—before you pay a single bill or sign a single check. Every bit of revenue yields profits every time. You're making profit both a priority and a habit.

2—Cut costs. Yeah, I know you've heard it before, but you need to hear it again. Whether you commit to wringing more out of the services and products you currently use, or you decide to eliminate certain expenses altogether, you can find ways to economize. Keep an open mind, and don't forget to keep your big picture goals in mind. Here's one example of a way I just discovered to cut costs, even though I thought my companies were pretty economical. We use Nextiva as our VOIP provider. We were also using a separate (and pricy) CRM service…until I learned that Nextiva has great CRM tools. I eliminated an unnecessary bill, improving my profitability.

3—Enlist the help of your staff. Once employees understand the relationship between a company's profitability and their personal goals and needs, they're much more willing to pitch in and keep an eye on your bottom line. Profit doesn't have to be a one-person job. Make use of your talented staff.

4—Be creative! You never know when inspiration can strike. My favorite tale about a newly profitable company is the Savannah Bananas, a minor league baseball team in Georgia. They were in a bad way, with huge debts and insane expenses, and they also needed a new ticketing system. The problem? These systems generally run in the neighborhood of $40,000. What did they do? The Bananas discovered they could print an entire season's worth of paper tickets for about $3,000, and since they made the tickets bright yellow and banana-shaped, people saved them as souvenirs, even posting pictures of them on social media. The Savannah Bananas got publicity, and saved a huge amount of money. A homerun for the Bananas!

5—Establish SMART profitability goals. If you don't have a goal, you'll never achieve it! Make sure you establish goals that are Specific, Measurable, Attainable, Realistic, and Time-Sensitive, and also make sure every member of your team understands those goals. Focusing on how each employee's performance relates to your SMART goals ensures your company stays focused and forward-thinking.

6—Take your profit personally. One of the strategies I teach when I'm advising entrepreneurs about making their companies profitable is to figure out how much income they need to live the lifestyle they desire. Once they've established their target income, we figure out how much revenue their company needs in order to hit that target. When you see your revenue goals as directly related to your income and your lifestyle, it makes profitability concrete—something you can touch, taste, smell, and enjoy.

Profit is not a dirty word, and in fact, being focused on profit doesn't mean that it's all about the money. Think about your company's profitability as a tool, a step toward achieving your goals. If your company is profitable, you and your employees can support families. If your company is profitable, then it can play a vital role in improving your community. If your company is profitable, it can continue providing outstanding service to your customers.

Putting your *Profit First* is what enables you to achieve goals, and it's the key to keeping your business healthy.

Mike Michalowicz is the author of Profit First.

RESOURCE:

Profit First: http://profitfirstbook.com/

HACK 44

HOW TO MAKE IT EASY FOR YOUR ACCOUNTANT TO FILE YOUR BUSINESS TAXES

MANY OWNERS NEVER learned how to file taxes for their companies. In fact, they dread the process of getting ready for the accountant and searching for the needed documentation. Many believe it as a confusing and arduous task that takes them away from running their businesses. They also see very little value in the activity except to satisfy the requirements of paying state and federal taxes.

Follow these steps to make it easier to get organized:

1—Review the company's profit and loss statement. If financial records have not been kept up to date, make sure that all revenue and expense transactions are entered correctly. The optimal way to do this is to balance these against the bank and credit card statements. Providing your accountant with an accurate profit and loss statement (and balance sheet) will make their job easier and ultimately less time consuming.

2—Check last year's tax return. This will make it simpler for you and your accountant to spot any obvious changes or errors that may be noted by the tax authorities. Comparing company results this year versus the previous year can also be a valuable financial management tool.

3—Decide the tax preparation method. Most companies have two choices: cash or accrual. Unless there is product inventory, most small businesses will opt to file their taxes on a cash basis since they only pay tax on money they have actually received, minus what was expensed. In some cases, a year-end listing of inventory and its value may be helpful to the accountant.

4—Download the journal from the outside payroll service (or internal accounting system). This should show all the W-2's sent employees for their individual taxes. It will also detail how much payroll tax was paid on their behalf and what was deducted from their paychecks.

5—Health insurance details. This may help satisfy federal requirements under the Affordable Care Act (still the law at press time) if the company has more than 50 employees.

6—Collect all 1099's sent to outside RESOURCES. Any non-employee that was paid more than $600 during the year needs to be sent a 1099-MISC form. These expenses should also be recorded on the company's profit and loss statement.

7—Sales tax paid. If the company is required to remit sales tax to state or local agencies, collect the documentation that shows those calculations and subsequent payments.

8—List of capital assets bought or sold. Any piece of equipment (or sometimes intellectual property) that is not able to be expensed in a single year needs to be depreciated on the balance sheet. Your accountant will need the name of the equipment (or expense) and when it was purchased.

9—Review documentation for travel and entertainment. These are typically heavily scrutinized by taxing authorities so detailed documentation on the exact purpose of the expense and who participated is critical.

10—Personal motor vehicle expenses used for business. This needs to include what the business purpose was, a log of miles traveled, and other operating expenses.

11—Summary of home office expenses. If your small business does not have an outside office, then sometimes a percentage of rent, home utilities, repairs, insurance, maintenance can be deducted from the business. Start by calculating the% of space the home office occupies times the total cost of maintaining the home last year.

12—Charitable donations. This needs to include the name of the charity, its appropriate legal status, and the exact amount of the donation.

13—Make copies of all quarterly business tax payments made on behalf of the corporation or by shareholders. This ensures your accountant properly credits these payments from the taxes that are finally due by companies or owners.

Why do all this? Correct records ensure all legal business expenses can be taken which will lower the tax that needs to be paid. If the corporation is an S or LLC, this tax return is required before the individual shareholders can file theirs. It will also make any audit by federal or state authorities much smoother. Finally, excellent preparation this year will make it easier to file taxes and get ready for the accountant next year!

RESOURCE

Difference between cash and accrual accounting:
http://www.investopedia.com/ask/answers/09/accrual-accounting.asp

HACK 45

HOW TO UNDERSTAND AND AVOID COMMON SALES AND USE TAX CHALLENGES

By Camille Mule`,

Owner, Proactive Accounting Solutions, LLC

SALES AND USE TAX compliance can be burdensome for any company because these taxes are complex, change constantly, and differ from state to state. The cost of non-compliance can be significant. This is true not only for the business itself, but for a business owner who can be held personally liable for sales and use tax due, even if the tax is not collected.

Quite often a business only learns of its sales and use tax responsibilities as the result of an audit. A costly audit can quickly put an end to your business and leave you in personal debt. But, by taking the following steps you can greatly reduce the chances of this happening to you.

1—Be proactive. Understand how sales and use tax applies to your business activities in the state/s where you conduct business. Implement a company wide sales and use tax policy and create a user-friendly manual for reference. Determine if your company is required to be registered in the state/s for sales tax purposes and register. Generally, registering for sales tax is a separate registration process, and is in addition to registering in a state for authority to do business in that state. In an e-commerce environment or if you conduct business from a brick-and-mortar location and make sales in multiple states, you'll need to be extra diligent in understanding and complying with each state's nexus rules. Also, in certain instances, many states' sales tax laws allow the state to hold the purchaser of an existing business responsible for any outstanding sales and use tax liabilities of the seller. Therefore, know what your responsibilities are. It is strongly advised you engage a sales tax advisor to assist you with these most important sales and use tax planning steps.

2—Maintain adequate books and records. The only way to know your financial position at all times is to maintain adequate books and records. This is needed to: make sound business decisions; avoid severe penalties imposed by taxing authorities for not keeping records; file tax returns; apply for credit; or defend your business in an audit. It also includes obtaining and maintaining properly completed exemption certificates, as required by most states, when tax is not collected at the time of sale.

3—File sales tax returns timely. Most states require returns be e-filed either monthly, quarterly, or annually depending upon sales or sales tax volume. In addition, most states require a return be filed even if there is no tax due. Avoid late filing penalties by timely filing returns. Automate your sales tax compliance function to increase accuracy and save time.

4—Design a Use Tax reporting system. In most states use tax is the complement of sales tax, and is imposed on the same taxable items at the same rate when sales tax is not paid at the time of purchase. Registered sales tax vendors are required to report and remit use tax when filing their sales tax return. In most states unregistered businesses must file an annual use tax report or a report for each occurrence. Even though your business may not have a sales tax obligation in a state (most states require sales tax registration only when a business sells taxable goods or services), it will have a use tax obligation as a purchaser. Having a reporting system in place allows you to avoid use tax challenges.

5—Self-audit on a regular basis. Sales transactions should be reviewed on a regular basis to ensure that sales tax is charged, and reported correctly on returns. Purchase transactions should also be reviewed occasionally as an efficient way to identify any potential overpayments of tax by your business on the goods and services it consumes.

6—Audit challenges. Being audited for sales and use tax is probably the most terrifying sales tax challenge. The best way to deal with this challenge is to engage a sales and use tax specialists who will be your best advocate. They know what your rights are, how the law applies to your business, and understand the auditing methods and techniques used by auditors. They also know how to interact and negotiate with auditors, limit an auditor's request for information, review purchase transactions for potential refund opportunities, and minimize any tax penalty and interest that may be due.

In summary, prevent sales and use tax challenges by keeping sales tax on your radar and make sure it is included as part of your overall tax planning strategy. Sales tax is a transaction tax, tax being collected at the time of the sale by the seller from the "ultimate customer". Don't shift this tax burden to your business, or worse yet yourself. Knowing what your responsibilities are, and complying accordingly is the best way to prevent sales and use tax challenges.

Camille Mule` is a multi-state sales and use tax consultant with over 30 years of experience helping clients, large and small, make sales and use tax part of their business strategies. She has worked for New York State as a tax audit supervisor, and as a state and local tax manager at a prominent national public accounting firm. Currently, she owns her own firm, Proactive Accounting Solutions, LLC.

HACK 46

HOW TO SURVIVE AN IRS AUDIT

By Manesh Makwana, Senior Tax Manager, CliftonLarsonAllen

THE WORST HAS HAPPENED. You're being audited by the Internal Revenue Service. The first thing to do is keep calm. Here are seven considerations you must know in order to successfully handle an IRS.

1—Know what to expect. IRS notices always come by mail. The letter will contain the IRS agent's name, badge number, a telephone number, and directions for how to schedule your first meeting. If anybody contacts you via phone or email to notify you of an audit, it might be a scam. Further into the process, the IRS agent may give you their IRS email address to electronically submit your documents, but generally IRS agents will not communicate through email.

2—Know your rights. It's important to know that the audit process gives you ample opportunity to assess and respond to the agent's findings. At your first meeting, the IRS agent will interview you about your business. Then they're send you an information document request (IDR). After you send them the requested documents, they will review them, and prepare a report outlining the things that aren't allowed under tax law, if there are any. The agent will send you the report to review. If you agree with the findings, follow the next steps as directed. If you disagree, you have the right to talk to a supervisor. The supervisor will work with the agent to reconcile the items you disagree on. If you still disagree with their assessment, you have the right to appeal.

3—Prepare, prepare, prepare. The IRS auditor's first focus will be your bank account transactions. They will look at your bank statements to see how your deposits and withdrawals compare to the income and expenses reported on your tax return. If your bank account shows $X and your tax return shows $Y, they're going to ask you about it. Be prepared to tell them why your tax return doesn't match the bank statements. Before your first meeting with the IRS agent, look at your deposits and expenses and match them to your tax returns so you know if there is a discrepancy or not.

4—Don't disclose more than you're asked for. In the first meeting interview, it is important to answer any questions as directly as possible without divulging too many details. Answer the questions truthfully, but the more detail you offer, the more the agent has to dig into.

5—Hire a pro. Hiring a professional accountant to represent you before the IRS is highly recommended. Since taxpayers don't often know the ins and outs of tax law, it's easy to get caught on IRS questions, and end up talking about things you shouldn't be talking about. It's always best to get a tax professional involved on the first day you get the audit notice.

6—Be responsive. Your first impression with the IRS agent is your last impression. If they see you're well organized, respectful, and providing information in a timely manner, the more favorable they will be. Even if you aren't ready with the information they need, communicate that to them and take an extension. For example, it's appropriate to tell them you're waiting for 60% of the information and will get it to them in two weeks. As long as they know you're engaged, they will be willing to work with you.

7—Do not lose your temper. If you do, they will use it against you in an effort to get you to reveal more problems that they can catch you on. Remember, you are not dealing with the "authorities". You are talking to a person who is representing the government, but they are not an authority, they're just an agent. They're also a human, and they're just doing their job.

Bottom line: If you're nervous about the process or you're not confident in your records, it's best to hire a professional accountant to represent you in the audit.

Manesh Makwana is a Senior Tax Manager with CliftonLarsonAllen (CLA) and over twenty years of experience in public accounting.

RESOURCE

CliftonLarsonAllen: http://www.claconnect.com/

HACK 47

HOW TO RAISE YOUR PRICES FOR MAXIMUM PROFIT

MOST SMALL BUSINESS OWNERS don't charge enough for their products or services. They typically undervalue what they offer customers due to fear. They want to raise their prices so they can increase their profits. But, they are afraid at a higher price, economics would force customers to buy less. The truth is, pricing is a lot more elastic than you think in business.

Here is how to raise your prices to get the most profit:

1—Don't sell a commodity. When customers can't differentiate between products which are available everywhere, they buy based on price. Small businesses have a difficult time building a profitable company selling these types of products. Stay away from building a company based on a commodity. Always think about how a customer will see your product as somehow different.

2—Don't compete on price. Using price as a marketing tactic is a race to the bottom with competitors. There will always be someone who can produce the product for less or is willing to cut their profits. Remember, you are in business not just to sell products, but to earn money doing it.

3—Sell value. Find the pain customers have and solve that. People pay for painkillers before they'll pay for vitamins. They'll also pay higher prices based on immediate need. For example, consumers routinely pay $4 for a bottle of water at movie theaters or $10 for a cocktail in a bar, although both are available at a grocery store for much less. Value (or perceived value) commands higher prices. Think premium brands like Apple and Harley Davidson. Or you can charge more by offering a better class of service, like the airlines offer their first-class passengers.

4—Watch competitors, but don't obsess about them. What do they charge? Track the value your company offers, compare it to theirs and make adjustments if necessary. It is always beneficial to ask customers who they think your competitors are so you understand the comparisons that are being made.

5—Bundle products or services. This can add value for customers that competitors can't compete with. It will also help to prevent channel conflict if you do not offer exactly what other dealers do.

6—Introduce price increases to new customers. The conventional wisdom is to charge existing customers more, and attract new customers by offering lower prices. This is wrong. Current customers deserve the best pricing to maximize their lifetime value. And current customers will become more loyal, if they know they're getting your best prices.

7—Add annual increases. Customers expect prices to always go up. Do it annually so you don't disappoint them!

8—Special circumstances produce temporary surcharges. Outside circumstance can necessitate a temporary rise in prices. Several years ago, for example, when wheat prices rose rapidly years ago, some restaurants added a surcharge on bread. While customers won't view surcharges as positive, if the issue the price raise is based on is widely accepted as a problem, they will accept it for a short period of time.

9—Pressure vendors for a lower price. Don't forget to focus on the other part of the profit equation: cost. Keeping all of a company's costs low will help the bottom line. Even if your profit goes up as a result of a price increase, ask vendors to lower your cost based on volume, payment terms or product substitution.

SALES HACKS

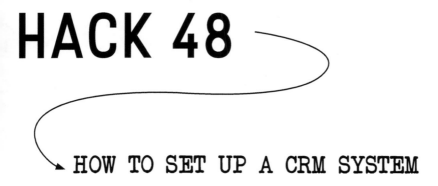

HACK 48

HOW TO SET UP A CRM SYSTEM

C RM STANDS FOR Customer Relationship Management, and no small business should be without it. CRM software enables you to capture information about prospects and customers, then analyze and act on that data. It automates the process by which you establish and maintain customer relationships.

CRM started out as contact management tool. Today's CRM software is so much more. According to Microsoft Dynamics 365, a strong CRM solution "is a multifaceted platform where everything crucial to developing, improving, and retaining your customer relationships is stored. Without the support of an integrated CRM solution, you may miss growth opportunities and lose revenue because you're not maximizing your business relationships."

While that sounds impersonal, CRM actually helps you be *more* personal with your customers. After all, the more you know about them and what they buy, the more they'll think you care about them as people, not just customers. And that will cement the bond between you and make them more loyal to your company.

Think of CRM as a business intelligence tool that not only helps you gather, centralize and analyze customer data, but enables you to automate marketing, track sales opportunities and improve your customer service.

There are numerous CRM systems to choose from. But before you decide to buy:

ASK YOURSELF THESE QUESTIONS:

1. What problems are you experiencing in your sales process? What challenges are you looking to solve? Do you need to access important data whenever and wherever you want? Or do you want one place to keep all customer information? Ask your staff what problems they've encountered with your sales process, as well.

2. Do you need something simple to get you through the startup stages of customer acquisition, or are you looking for more of a customer retention tool?

3. How many employees do you have who need to use the system?

4. What is your budget for CRM?

5. Do you have an IT person on staff who can help if something goes wrong or you're having problems figuring something out?

ASK THE CRM COMPANY:

1. How many employees can use the system, and can it scale with my business?

2. Are there different features available at different price levels?

3. Is the system completely mobile-friendly?

4. What kind of security does the system have so my customers' information is safe?

5. How easy is the system to learn? Is there a tutorial available? Do you offer training?

6. What kind of support is available if you have questions or there's a problem? Does that support consist of more than online FAQs? Will a real person get back to you in a timely manner?

7. Once the customer information is entered, is the information available offline as well as online?

8. What other programs does the CRM tool integrate with, such as accounting and email systems?

9. What special features are available, such as direct calling and

emailing from the system, or social networking features?

10. What kinds of reports can be generated from the system? What real-time alerts can be set up?

11. How easy is it to transfer the information to another system if you aren't satisfied with the one you chose?

There's a CRM system for every size business—and practically every budget. And the ROI you get from investing in CRM is well worth it.

RESOURCE

Microsoft Dynamics 365: https://www.microsoft.com/en-us/dynamics365/what-is-crm

HACK 49

HOW TO MAKE A COLD CALL

By Wendy Weiss, President, ColdCallingResults.com

MOST SMALL BUSINESS OWNERS either think cold calling is dead, it doesn't work, or they just don't want to do it. Follow these five steps to discover how cold calling absolutely does work and why you should be doing it.

1—Understand what cold calling isn't. There is a myth that cold calling involves opening the phone book, calling anybody, saying anything, and hoping as long as you make hundreds of dials a day, eventually someone will say yes. If that's the strategy you're employing, it's true, cold calling won't work. Cold calling is about sharing a carefully crafted message with a very specific group of people.

Many people think you can just send emails or use social media to engage with prospects, but that's actually unlikely to get you very far. A University of Chicago study on the effectiveness of written communication (emails, social media, a letter) versus spoken communication (telephone conversation, voicemail or in person) revealed if someone hears your voice, even if it's just in a voicemail, three things happen. they think you're smarter, they're more engaged, and they're more likely to take action than if they just read something. It is absolutely worth your time to pick up the phone and talk to your prospects.

2—Profile your ideal prospect. The answer to "Who should I call?" is—not everybody. Before you get on the phone, put together a profile of exactly who it is that you're targeting. Determine your ideal prospect's industry, revenue, number of employees, and geographic location. If you're targeting the consumer market, determine your best prospect's age, marital status, number of children, and income level. A parameter such as "the company should have between 10 and 5000 employees" is too broad. The business owner of a company with 10 employees is going to have much different issues than the head of HR at a company with 5000 employees. Be specific!

3—Stop making excuses. Many small business owners don't cold call because they believe prospects won't take their call. Actually, there are a lot of reasons prospects *will* take your call. If you've done your homework and you've put together a strong prospect list, they need what you're offering. Also, it's their job to know what's out there, what the best resources are, and what the industry's prices are, so when you call a prospect and introduce yourself, you're actually helping them do their job.

4—Prepare what you're going to say. Once you've established who you're calling, you must figure out what you're going to say. Start by determining goal for the conversation. Be realistic—your goal should not be to get the prospect to dump their vendor in the 60 seconds they're on the phone with you. Your goal should be to get the prospect's agreement to have a more in-depth conversation with you. This might happen over the phone, face-to-face, in person or in an online meeting.

5—Know how to handle rejection. The formula for responding to any objection is 1) Agree with them. It doesn't matter what they say, they are right. 2) Reframe what they just said. 3) Ask for meeting again. If they say, "I'm already working with someone", respond "I understand you're already working with someone. Right now, I'd simply like to introduce myself and if your situation changes, you'll know me. Can we talk next week?" It's a simple formula that far too many sales professionals do not use.

If you hear "I'm not interested", you're not talking to the right person. If you don't have a good prospect list, you will hear this a lot; they're really not buying what you're selling. If you're calling larger companies, you'll hear this if you haven't targeted the decision maker. In this case, they're really saying, "I have nothing to do with this decision". If you're sure you're talking to the right people and you hear, "I'm not interested", you're simply not saying anything they find interesting. What you say has to be relevant to the person you're saying it to. That's true in prospecting and in life.

Successful cold calling is all about saying the right things to the right people, and if you do that, you will see why it's such a powerful sales method.

Wendy Weiss is the Cold Call Queen.

RESOURCE
Cold Calling Results: http://www.coldcallingresults.com/

HACK 50

HOW TO MAKE A SALES CALL

By Anthony Iannarino,
Entrepreneur, Speaker & Bestselling Author

S ELLING IS A COMPLEX, dynamic human interaction. There are a lot of ways to have different conversations with many possible outcomes.

1—Say thank you. You should open a sales call by thanking your prospective customer for their time. You don't need to look around the room to find something you can use to connect with the buyer, like pictures of their kids or their hobbies. Just say, *"Thank you for meeting with me."*

2—Set the agenda. The most professional and effective way to start a sales call is by sharing your agenda. You want to tell your prospective customer what you intend to do with the time they are giving you.

If you need to learn about your prospect and their business, say, *"I hope we can spend a few minutes getting a better understanding of what you do and how we might help."* If you are meeting to present your product, service, or solution, say, *"We want to show you what we do, and we want to explain how we believe it will benefit you."*

3—Share what comes next. A lot of people believe "closing" is something that happens at the very end of the sales process. The truth is you are always asking for the commitments that help you to serve your clients and help them achieve their goals and outcomes.

You want to tell your prospect where you hope to go by letting them know what comes next. Say, "*At the end of this meeting, if it makes sense for you, we'll schedule another appointment (or prepare a proposal).*" Or, if you need to have another meeting to learn more, tell your prospect that by saying, "*We'll still need to come back and do more work when we are done here today. So, if this works for you, we'll schedule that next meeting before we leave.*" Setting the stage for what comes next makes it easier to gain that commitment later. Your prospect may have needs of their own. You must check before diving into your agenda.

4—Ask for modifications. You are here to serve your prospective client. You want to make sure they are tracking with your agenda, and get what they need. Ask, "*Does this work for you, or is there something else that you'd like to add?*" If your prospect wants something, they will tell you, and you can make sure they get what they need.

5—The sales conversation. Once you've gained agreement on the agenda, the execution of a sales call is simply a conversation. The more conversational, the better. It's just a couple of people talking.

If you are sitting across from your prospective client because you need to do the discovery work that allows you to supply them with what they need, ask the questions that allow you to gather that information. The better your questions, the better the sales call. You want your questions to demonstrate you have insight and ideas.

If the goal of your meeting is to present or pitch your product, service or solution, start by telling your prospect where they are now, where you believe they are going, and how you can help them get there. This is a dialogue, not a monologue. You want to show your prospect you know how to get them to the better future state they need, and you are the right person to get them there.

6—Closing the call. After having the sales conversation that makes up the bulk of your call, you should gain the agreement to take the next step together. That next step is likely another sales call. Like the rest of the sales conversation, your close should be very natural—you don't need to say anything weird.

Say, "*Thank you for your time today. The next thing we need to do is get back together to show you a few options, and provide you with a proposal. What do you look like Thursday afternoon?*"

If what you sell can be sold in a single call, close by asking for the business. "*It looks like what we discussed today is a perfect fit for you. Can I go ahead and set up your account and get your started?*"

Anthony Iannarino is an International speaker, the bestselling author of The Only Sales Guide You'll Ever Need, a sales leader, and entrepreneur. He blogs daily at The Sales Blog and posts daily on his YouTube channel.

Resources

The Sales Blog: https://thesalesblog.com/

YouTube: www.youtube.com/iannarino

HACK 51

HOW TO GET A PROSPECT TO RESPOND (WHEN THEY WON'T)

THERE ARE MANY TIMES a prospect says they are interested, want a proposal or they're ready to buy. Then, when you contact them, you hear nothing. Here's how to get them to at least respond so you can move forward with the sales process or move to the next prospect.

Email Title. Should we really work together?

Dear Sara,

I have been unsuccessful in my attempts to reach you and provide the information you requested. This typically means.

> *1. You've just been busy but are still very interested in talking with me about how I can help.*

> *2. You are no longer interested, and I should stop trying to contact you.*

As a businessperson, I know you can appreciate the position I'm in, because you want to know similar answers from your customers. I want to provide you with excellent customer service and all the information you require to make an educated decision that will benefit your business. What I don't want to do is bother you with something if you are no longer interested.

Could you please help both of us by letting me know which of the two situations we are in? This will allow me to better allocate my time while still providing you with the amount of attention you desire.

Thanks again,

Barry

With this letter, you will get a response 80% of the time from the prospect. This works because it encourages the prospect to say "no" in simple business terms they understand. This lets them off the sales hook easily if they were afraid of saying "no" after saying "sort of yes" or after not replying to you for a long time. Remember, it is far too costly to try to do business with anyone who doesn't truly want to do business with you.

There is another letter that can be used that we found from Pam Slim, who helps small businesses grow. She uses an A, B, C format similar to this one.

Email Title. Please Reply A, B, or C

Dear Zane,

I have been unsuccessful in connecting with you. Can you simply reply with one letter, A, B, or C?

A. I am still interested in working with you. Let's set a date to talk.

B. I have been busy. Please follow up with me in a few weeks since I am still interested.

C. Thanks for your time. Things have changed and I am no longer interested in talking.

Thank you.

Rieva

Even if they are busy, they can reply with one letter.

To increase the odds of a reply to 95%, there is a slightly riskier letter you can send. At this stage, however, I recommend using it since there is not much to lose.

Email Title. I thought you were dead!

Dear Daniel,

I really don't know what else to say. I thought we had some good conversations about working together. I am personally surprised and a bit disappointed I have not heard from you. Maybe you are no longer at Pennewig Company, or you are sick or were in a serious accident. These different possibilities make me worry about you.

At this point, I am less concerned about doing business together, but let me know that you are OK or if you have taken a job at a different company.

Thanks for taking the time to respond,

Barry

Remember that any response is the ultimate goal. You may not do business with this prospect, but you will get a reply, and this will help you move onto other prospects. On the small chance that none of these methods generate a reply, cross them off your active list.

HACK 52

HOW TO HIRE A MANUFACTURERS' REP

WHEN YOU START A BUSINESS, you may be the only salesperson you can afford. But at some point, if you want to grow, you're going to need to hire salespeople. First, you need to decide if you want to hire in-house sales staff or outside sales reps.

Manufacturers' reps are independent salespeople who represent several clients, usually in a specific industry. You want to hire someone who sells complementary, not competitive products.

For startups and small businesses, hiring manufacturers' reps can save you money, since they're paid on commission-only. Plus, they work from their own offices, so you don't have to pay any overhead, which is particularly ideal if you run your business from your home.

Reps also bring with them their vast industry knowledge and contacts, so they can help a new business break into a new industry (this also helps existing businesses that are launching new product lines).

How do you find manufacturers' reps? You can start here.

» Get referrals from colleagues

» Ask buyers for recommendations

» Attend trade shows

» Advertise in industry magazines or websites

» Contact a manufacturers' rep association (Try the Manufacturers'

Agents National Association and your industry-specific rep associations.)

When you interview a potential rep, make sure they aren't carrying too many product lines—it's important your rep has enough time to focus on your business—and don't sell competitive products.

Selling your products is a crucial function, so your rep must be trustworthy and dependable. Be sure to contact references and do an online search to learn more about their background and reputation. Also, look at their social media accounts—you don't want to hire someone who will later embarrass you.

A caveat for startups—manufacturers' reps rarely take on brand-new businesses. You might need to grow your sales to a certain level before they'll take you on.

Remember, reps are independent contractors so you can't directly control how they do their jobs. To protect your business, create a thorough contract which specifically spells out what you expect from the rep, how their performance will be evaluated, their territory and their compensation package. Specify the circumstances under which the rep can be terminated.

It's important to stay in regular contact with your reps. Keep them up-to-date on new products and innovations. And ask them for feedback on how your products are perceived in the marketplace.

RESOURCE

Manufacturers' Agents National Association: https://www.manaonline.org/

HACK 53

HOW TO HIRE IN-HOUSE SALES STAFF

I F YOU PREFER TO HIRE in-house sales personnel, just posting a job and asking for resumes is not enough. A friend of mine once shared how he "sorts out" sales applicants. He posts ads, asks for resumes and then waits for the applicants to call him first. This, he swears, identifies the people who aren't afraid to make cold calls.

When you do interview the applicants, look for the people who come prepared, who've done their research about you, your business and your industry. You'll also want to make sure the person listens as much as talks and asks smart questions.

You can't expect to just hire salespeople and expect them to succeed. You need:

1—A sales strategy. How many salespeople are you hiring? How will you split up sales territories? Will you give your sales staff quotas? What's the compensation plan? Bonus structure? Will they work out of the main office? Their homes? Will you give them company cars? These are just a few of the questions you need to address.

It's smart to create a "sales handbook" that lays out the answers to the above questions and more. You need to clearly spell out your expectations and set goals, whether they be daily, weekly, monthly or quarterly.

2—Sales management. If you hire more than one salesperson, who will they report to? You can't just hire a sales staff and let them loose without any supervision. Do you have the time to deal with them every day and still accomplish what you need to as the owner of the company? If not, you'll need to hire an experienced sales manager to oversee your staff. Make sure you have the ongoing sales to support this type of infrastructure.

3—Sales training. To be effective, sales training should be an ongoing process. Best practices call for a minimum of two weeks of sales training for new salespeople. They need to learn about your products, pricing, technology and the competition. Some may need to brush up on their sales skills. Many companies have quarterly sales training meetings, where the staff shares best practices, discusses what is and isn't working for them, shores up any weak spots and gets updates about what your competitors are up to.

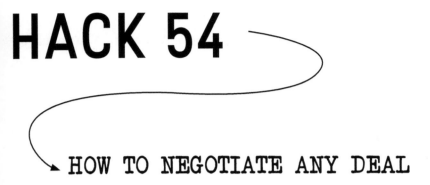

HACK 54

HOW TO NEGOTIATE ANY DEAL

Negotiating is a key skill every business owner needs to learn. Here are 10 tactics that are used all the time, how you can spot them, and what to do about it.

1—Left at the altar. This is when the other party feigns backing out of a deal right before the agreement is to be completed. It's hoped for effect is to bring the other party closer to their position yielding 11th hour concessions. **Your countermeasure:** Don't fall for the bait! Let the deal drop and go through a quiet period. Try resurrecting the deal in no less than 30 days or when they call you. At that point, it will be your turn to get concessions.

2—Making balloon futures. The other party is forecasting future sales growth which are accelerated from historic averages. This is similar to "The Call Girl Principle" where a service is worth more before it's performed. **Your countermeasure:** Base your decision or price only on past history. Make available future bonuses or payouts contingent on if accelerated growth actually happens.

3—Calling a higher authority. The other party says they are unable to make a final decision or won't tell you who the final decision maker is. **Your countermeasure:** Stop negotiating until you are discussing directly with that decision maker. You are wasting your time.

4—Crunch time. The other party applies a lot of pressure by saying, "That's nonsense, you have to do much better than that." **Your countermeasure:** Use "the Flinch" tactic by showing shock and amazement this has been brought up. Repeat the offer you just made.

5—Bring in the dancer. This is when a member of the other party talks for a long time without saying anything substantive to the real issues. This is usually used as a distraction. This can also be a "snow job" bringing unnecessary data to support the other party's position. **Your countermeasure:** Ask, "Specifically, what does this have to do with what we are talking about?" Repeat several more times if necessary.

6—Retrading the deal. Attempting to reopen any points in the negotiation after agreement has been reached. Also called, "forgotten issue". **Your countermeasure:** Simply say no. Call them out for breaking the agreement. This may turn into "left at the altar" (See #1).

» **Huntley and Brinkley**. Two people for the other party teaming up against you at the same time. **Your countermeasure:** If you can't handle the pressure, get someone to join you or ask to negotiate with only one person at a time.

» **Turning Soviet**. A really mean negotiator who doesn't care if the other side gets anything out of the deal. **Your countermeasure:** Ask for someone else to negotiate with and don't start again until your request is granted.

» **The walkout**. Deliberately walking out of a negotiation to show disinterest. **Your countermeasure:** Let them walk out. If they do not come back, leave. Do not call them for a month.

» **Roaring brains**. These are people who talk a lot with no real experience in a particular area. **Your countermeasure:** Do the research, and have the facts to question their experience and data.

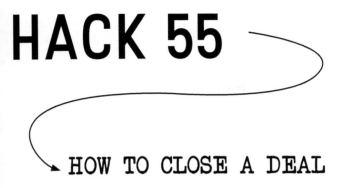

HACK 55

HOW TO CLOSE A DEAL

THERE ARE MANY ATTRIBUTES good salespeople have, but perhaps none is more important than the ability to close a deal. So, is there a secret formula to successfully closing a deal? Sorry to say no, but here are some things you should consider.

1— Are you talking to the right person? You may need to work your way up the chain, but you can't close a deal, unless you're talking to the decision maker. You never want to be rude or dismissive, but you need to work your way through the gatekeeper to the person who has the power to say "yes".

2—Timing is everything. Some companies may not want to make deals in the last month of their fiscal years. Others may have distinct buying cycles. You don't want to waste your time trying to close a deal that cannot be closed for months. Of course, you can always plant seeds at these times.

3— Set deadlines. While you might be working on a tight deadline, your prospects likely don't share that sense of urgency. This is when you need to up your sales game. Some clients need to be wooed to pull the trigger. Others, especially those who've never done business with you before, may need assurance you're the real deal. (Testimonials come in handy here.)

Is there something you can offer to sweeten the deal? Discounts? Exclusivity? Limited time offer?

The key is to figure out why the prospect is hesitating (Price? Timing? Not comfortable with you?), and address that particular factor.

4—Be helpful. During the "courting" stage, it's important to do more than just sell the prospect. Show them you're investing in their success. Send them articles, trends or other information that can help them do their jobs. The more helpful you are, the more they'll learn to trust you—and we all know people prefer to do business with people they know, like and trust.

5—Getting to the "yes". So, how do you actually get to the yes? Every top salesperson has key phrases or questions they swear by. HubSpot, one of my favorite sites, compiled a list of their favorite "closing phrases to seal the sales deal." Here are a few.

1. "Is there any reason, if we gave you the product at this price, that you wouldn't do business with our company?"

2. "If we throw in [freebie], would that convince you to sign the contract today?"

3. "Taking all of your requirements and desires into consideration, I think these two products would work best for you. Would you like to go with [X] or [Y]?"

4. "So, when should we get started on implementation?"

5. "Why don't you give it/us a try?"

RESOURCE

Hubspot closing phrases: https://blog.hubspot.com/sales/closing-phrases-seal-sales-deal#sm.00044ru1bk4ndy310qa1ene9m6kjw

MARKETING HACKS

HACK 56

HOW TO USE EMAIL MARKETING

By Ramon Ray, Speaker & Entrepreneur

O NE OF THE MOST cost-effective ways to grow a small business today is through email marketing. It gives you the ability to not only attract your ideal clients and customers, but to then speak to them in a very personal way, and deliver content specific to their interests. Personalization and targeting go a long way in turning a simple prospect into a life-long customer.

Whether you are just starting out or looking to boost your efforts, there are some key strategies you should consider to create an effective and successful email marketing program for your business.

CHOOSING AN EMAIL MARKETING PROGRAM

There is no shortage of email marketing programs you can choose from, ranging from the very simple such as Constant Contact, MailChimp, and Emma to more complex Customer Relationship Management (CRM) programs like Insightly, Aweber, and Infusionsoft. The key is to find one that has the key functionality you need, and fits within your small business budget. Some features to consider would include.

- » Simple design tools
- » Automation (autoresponders, campaigns)
- » CAN-SPAM compliance

» Contact segmentation

» Customer Relationship Management (CRM) and social media integration

» Mobile responsive

» A/B testing

» Analytics and reporting

BUILDING YOUR LIST

Once you have chosen your email marketing program, it is time to start finding prospects and building your list. There are several effective ways to build a list including.

» **Add a subscription box to your website.** If you have managed to attract someone to your website, now is the time to capture them by inviting them to subscribe to your list. You can do this with simple sign-up boxes, or free information offers placed on your site with a clear Call-to-Action (CTA).

Pro Tip: Don't make people search for a way to join your list! Keep subscription offers up front and place them on each of your key website pages.

» **Add subscription offers to social media.** Ask your followers across your social channels to subscribe to your list or make your lead generation offers available on the various platforms for quick and easy sign-up.

» **Encourage sharing.** The people currently on your list are already fans, so encourage them to share your information with their friends and contacts. You can do this by including a link in each email you send that allows them to share specific content via email or on their social channels.

Pro Tip. Not everyone joins your list for the same reasons. This is where segmentation comes into play. Have a strategy to 'tag' subscribers to your list based on various aspects, including how they subscribed, the type of content or products they are interested in, geography, demographics, etc. By thinking about segmentation when you start, you will have more options for target marketing down the road.

Anatomy of a Successful Email

Once you start seeing more and more subscribers join your list, the hard part starts—keeping them on your list and engaged. This is where many small businesses fail. However, there are some key strategies you can put in place to help increase your success, including.

» **Valuable and relevant content.** People joined your list because you have information they crave, so give it to them. Make sure your content is relevant to what your audience wants and deliver it in various ways including text, graphics, and videos. Always aim to be informative versus 'salesy' and include a call-to-action in all content driving people back to one of your online assets (website, social, products, etc.).

» **A killer subject line.** The number-one goal of email marketing is to achieve a high open rate and that all rests on having a subject line that entices and intrigues people to open the email. Subject lines should be short and sweet (30–50 characters) and grab your audience's attention without being misleading.

» **Get personal.** Research shows personalized email messages improve click-through rates by an average of 14% and conversions by 10%. Additionally, emails with personalized subject lines are about 26% more likely to be opened.

Key email elements. Ensure each email contains some key elements, including.

» Branded 'send from' email associated with your business

» Clear CTA's that direct people to take the actions you desire

- » Professional closing and signature that includes contact information
- » Include a link for the subscriber to either update their information or unsubscribe in the footer

TIMING AND TESTING

You can find a ton of information on what the best days and times are to send your emails, but ultimately it depends on your specific audience. This is where testing becomes effective. Try sending your emails on different days at various times, and then monitor your open-rates to see when you get the best response.

Other variables you should consider testing include.

- » Subject lines
- » Format (HTML vs. Plain Text)
- » Call-to-Actions

ANALYTICS

Analytics play a vital part in a successful email marketing program, and it is essential you continually monitor your data to ensure you are optimizing your efforts. Some key metrics to watch include.

- » Open rates
- » Click-through rates
- » Unsubscribe rates
- » Hard / soft bounce rates
- » Forward /Share rates

RESOURCES

Ramon Ray: http://www.ramonray.com/

Email marketing programs

Constant Contact: https.//www.constantcontact.com/home

MailChimp: https.//mailchimp.com/

Emma: http://myemma.com/

Insightly: https.//www.insightly.com/

Aweber: https.//www.aweber.com/

Infusionsoft: https.//www.infusionsoft.com/

HACK 57

HOW TO WRITE EMAILS THAT GET OPENED

OVER 200 BILLION emails are sent every day. It's tough to get your emails to stand out from all the noise—even if it has great content. Here is what to do to boost your open rates to at least 25%.

1—The subject line. The subject or title of your email is what determines whether people open your email. Remember, you don't have to give everything away in that first line. In 2012, when former President Obama used email marketing for fundraising, his most successful title used was simply "Hey." Others that work are "referred by," "our appointment this week," and "I am waiting for your call."

2—Be provocative. Would the title make you open an email? Last year, one of my most popular email titles was, "My wife thinks I am having an affair." When the email was opened, the article talked about how I wasn't home a lot because I was working on my small business.

3—Go negative. Unfortunately, titles with negative words have higher open rates. Use phrases like "the worst," "absolutely wrong," and "no fewer." As an example, one of my emails that had a very high open rate this year had the subject line, "5 Reasons Why Stupid People Make More Money than You."

4—Be exclusive. Words and terms like "VIP," "exclusive," "invitation," "limited time," and "the deadline is Thursday" draw people in and make them act. Everyone wants to be part of the club! Use a title like "Exclusive Invitation to …"

5—No capital letters. In the world of email, using all capital letters is like SCREAMING AT THE PERSON, which is never considered proper business etiquette. Also, emails with too many words in all caps are likely to get flagged by spam filters.

6—Be controversial about current event topics (but not political). Take a contrarian viewpoint, as long as it's something that makes sense for your brand, and you're genuine about your take on the position. For example, if the general consensus among your readers is a higher minimum wage is bad, post arguments to the contrary for the content to get read.

7—Avoid these words. Never use the words "free," "help," "percent off," and "reminder." These are overused email titles and will negatively affect open rates.

8—Use numbers. People are lazy when it comes to learning new things. Who has time to read nine paragraphs of information, when that same information can be distilled down to nine neat bullet points? If your title promises your readers will learn a lot in a little time, people will check it out.

> ***Pro Tip.*** *Using odd numbers and the number 10 in titles can boost open rates.*

9—Keep it short. More than 50% of email is opened on mobile devices. Many smartphones cut off titles at 25 characters. Use a tool like

Litmus, which checks how a subject line and email will actually appear in prospects' inboxes based on the device they're using.

10—Get help. If you have difficulty creating titles, there are tools that can help. Tweak Your Biz provides a title generator to improve open rates.

11—Don't forget the "from" field. The email should always come from a person at the company. If possible, it should be from the most recognizable person that registers with the audience you're sending it to. Never send an email from just "the company," "info" or "sales." It's too impersonal, and almost all but guarantees a low open rate.

RESOURCE

Tweak Your Biz: http://tweakyourbiz.com/

HACK 58

HOW TO CREATE A SOCIAL STRATEGY FOR YOUR BUSINESS

BY BRIAN MORAN, ADVISOR, CONSULTANT & ENTREPRENEUR

ONE OF THE BIGGEST mistakes business owners make when it comes to social media is they don't put together a plan for making it work. Often, I've seen companies dabble in LinkedIn, Facebook or Twitter only to claim it didn't do anything after using it for a month or two. This approach to social media has to stop. If you want to make your business relevant, it's time to create a social strategy that works.

Small businesses can no longer ignore the conversations, reviews and purchases taking place on various social media channels. Your customers and prospects are posting pictures on Instagram, writing reviews on Yelp, and talking to friends about their experiences and/or potential purchases on Facebook, Twitter, Snapchat and Pinterest.

To create a winning social media strategy, you will need persistence, patience and a focused effort. Here are five ways social media can help grow your business.

1—Connect with customers and prospects. Social media is a platform to market your products and/or services in a non-invasive, educational manner. Ask your existing customers if they want to engage with your company on social media. You can let them know about special programs, discounts, and changes in your business through various social channels. If they opt to add your company to their social networks, listen to what they are discussing and engage with them when applicable. Share content, answer questions, and congratulate them if they post good news. The more you engage with customers and prospects, the deeper your relationship becomes with them. Consider how you can help them achieve their desired results and how that connects to your unique value proposition.

2—Conduct market research. Benchmarking is one of the best ways to remain current on changes in your industry. Social media offers insights into the future of your business and marketplace. By following industry influencers, media people covering your market, and experts, you have immediate access to data that simply wasn't available before the rise of social media.

In addition to understanding the many changes in your industry, social media can help you find answers to tough questions. If you struggle with a particular problem, social media should be one of your first "go to" resources. Use sites such as Facebook, Twitter or LinkedIn to conduct surveys or ask people for their comments on specific opportunities or overcoming obstacles. Think of these platforms as boards of advisors ready to help you manage and grow your business.

3—Network with experts, influencers, and media. Whenever I attend a trade show or conference, I always put together a list of key people I want to meet at the event. The list usually includes someone from the media, an industry expert or two, and people who are influential in that particular industry (e.g. a blogger or someone with a large following on one of the social media platforms). Before attending the event, I connect and engage with everyone on one or more social platforms. The prep work turns a cold call into a warm introduction. The engagements give me access to smart people while expanding my network. In turn, I share information I've gathered on their particular industries.

4—Track your competitors. Social media can help you virtually track your competition. In the course of a week, your competitors will post pictures from events they attended, tweet about client meetings, and write blog posts about new products or services they plan to offer. On LinkedIn, you can track new hires and recent layoffs simply by doing a company search (LinkedIn is one of the first platforms updated by employees when changing jobs).

5—Build your brand. Everything you do on social media has an impact, positive or negative, on your brand. It is imperative to be mindful of your blog posts, tweets, posted pictures, and status updates and how they are helping you build your brand. The simple rule is, "Don't post something on social media you wouldn't say or show to someone in person."

Time is the biggest investment you will make in social media. Instead of looking at ROI (Return on Investment), you should measure R.O.T.I. (Return on Time Invested). If your business is new to social media, start with the one platform that is most popular with your target audience. Learn how to successfully build a solid foundation and then use that platform to connect with people on other social platforms. Before you know it, social media will be the core component of your successful marketing strategy.

Brian Moran is an award-winning global advisor to entrepreneurs, business owners, and companies interested in targeting the small to midsize business market. He spent 20+ years publishing magazines and newspapers for business owners, and sits on the board of directors for several entrepreneurial organizations.

RESOURCE

Small Business Edge: http://smallbusinessedge.com/

HACK 59

HOW TO GET STARTED WITH SEARCH ENGINE OPTIMIZATION (SEO)

By Ryan Cantor, Assistant VP Digital, DexYP

ANY SMART LOCAL BUSINESS owner would love to appear at the top of the list when local customers search for their products or services online. The key to doing that—aside from buying ad space—comes down to search engine optimization (SEO). This basically means setting your website up so that search engines like it and want to point consumers to it. Using essential keywords and incorporating quality links on your site helps your business rise in search engine rankings. But, SEO is truly a science.

Though SEO has evolved in recent years, don't waste your time looking for an SEO quick fix. The core principles of successful SEO are dependable and unwavering. and you don't need slick tricks to get found online. It boils down to relevance and trust. Content you share on your own website, when coupled with your broader online presence gets it done. Search engines rank your company's website based on authentic, relevant content. Not only are they really good at it, they see right past SEO gimmicks that try to shortcut authentic SEO work.

Here are the basics, boiled down to just two key actions.

1—Put the time in and do your onsite work.

» **Tell your story.** Search engines like Google optimize their results to best suit consumer needs. This means you need in-depth, relevant, appropriate content based on what you want to be found for. Typically, 250-400 words per service you offer, each on its own, separate page, will make your website rank as more relevant and reliable in the eyes of the Google gods.

» **Talk about what you offer in terms people use when they search.** No one searches single keywords any more. This means keyword stuffing (which was never really a stellar idea in the first place) is obsolete. Now, it's all about keyword phrases made up of three to four words. "Cleaners" becomes, "Dry cleaners with drive-thru." "Groomer" becomes, "Groomer specializing in poodles."

» **Structure your website correctly.** You've got to use clean code that is logical and reader-focused. That makes it easy to write, edit and maintain your site long-term. Don't stress if you're not a coding savant—there's a lot of help out there.

» **Go mobile.** Last year, more searches took place on mobile devices than on computers. To cater to these users, search engines love mobile-optimized websites. If your site isn't mobile-friendly or mobile-responsive, you'll rank much lower in search results.

2—Don't neglect the rest of the online space.

» **Talk about your product or service outside your own website.** Doing so will position you as an authority in your industry. This builds trust, not only with potential and current customers, but with search engines as well.

» **Where do I start?** Become an active contributor to blogs (your own or someone else's), industry articles, online listings and business profiles, social bookmarks and more. Getting your business's name out there as a thought leader positions you as an authority and creates trust.

Pro Tip. *Be real, and keep it fresh. Ultimately, being found is about conversion. Getting found for the wrong reasons is useless. Search engines are working all day, every day, to refine their mechanisms to deliver the most relevant content. So, while it's awesome to be found, you want to be found for the right reasons. Find ways to incrementally add content, if possible from your customers. Reviews, feedback, testimonials, blogs, updated photos (with all meta data and alt tags intact) are great ways to keep your online content fresh, evolving and relevant.*

Ryan Cantor is the Assistant Vice President of Digital for DexYP. He leads the company's non-advertising digital products and business services.

RESOURCE

www.dexyp.com

HACK 60

HOW TO DO SEARCH ENGINE MARKETING

By Faith Murphy, Senior Director of Sales, Oath

BEFORE YOU BEGIN search engine marketing, you must have a mobile responsive website. Users consume content and search on multiple platforms, including desktops, tablets, and phones, and your website must be formatted specially for all three devices. Once you have a responsive website, follow these seven steps to create your search engine marketing campaign.

1—Know what goals you're trying to achieve. What are you trying to achieve with search engine marketing? Are you trying to sell a product? Do you want people to sign up for your newsletter? Do you want people to call you to schedule your service? Before you start putting any money into a campaign, determine what your ultimate goal is.

2—Identify your ideal target. What types of customers have you had repeated success with? This is the ideal target for your campaign. If you're a yoga studio, perhaps your ideal customers are moms wanting to get fit. As you start to create your campaign, your goal is to build messaging that will resonate with this persona.

3—Implement an analytics program. It's important to have a good analytics program such as Google Analytics installed on your website before you start running marketing campaigns. Google Analytics tracks which search engine your traffic is coming from, and shows you the overall performance of your campaign, which will help you make future decisions. Now you can start to build your campaigns.

4—Identify your keywords. Choose keywords from each of the three parts of the sales funnel. The top level of the sales funnel is awareness and it contains people who aren't familiar with your business. To target this group, choose broad keywords that describe who you are and what you do, like "plumber". The middle level of the funnel contains people who have already started to home in on the product they're after. They're in the engaging and considering phase, and focused on information gathering. If you're a plumber, these keywords could be "kitchen remodel" or "bathroom remodel". The third level of the funnel contains people who are buyers and ready to make a purchase. These keywords are focused on action, and are often the most descriptive, for example "Emergency plumber in Los Angeles, California".

5—Write ad copy. After you've identified your keywords, write ad copy that talks to all three stages of the sales funnel. With the high-level keywords, describe your business so people can get to know you. For the middle keywords, be more specific by calling out specific services you offer, such as kitchen remodel quotes. Lastly, for the people who have their credit cards out, give them a reason to click through to your website and buy; give them your price point, and share that you offer free consultations, for example. For each ad, make sure you have a landing page that reflects what you just told them. If your ad is about plumbing remodels, bring them to a page with photos, a blurb about what remodeling entails, and the average cost. This content must be in place on your website first, and will oftentimes drive the focus of your ad.

6—Target your audience. I recommend being restrictive with your target audience at first. If you go big and broad right away, you're probably going to spend a ton of money and not see many results. If your business does mortgages, you don't want to target teens, so narrow it to ages 25-35. If you only service a certain city, then only target that city. If you want more exposure, do state-level targeting and add keywords for your city specifically. In order to target your audience, you should be clear on who your ideal customer is.

7—**Set your budget.** The great thing about search engine marketing is that it's an auction model, that is, you get to set your pricing. First and foremost, consider your costs of doing business. If you sell a pencil for a dollar, you probably shouldn't be bidding a dollar per click; you will make 0 dollars. If a lawyer makes $25,000 on a case, they're comfortable spending $40-$50 per click to win the auction for highly competitive keywords. Also, be strategic with how much you bid for each specific keyword. If purple Nike sneakers are the best seller on your website, then bid aggressively on those keywords because those are good profit keywords for you. Also, each advertising platform has forecasting tools available, so utilize those to understand the marketplace you are in.

Give a new campaign two weeks before making a decision on whether it's performing for you. At that time, review your initial goals and begin to tweak components of your campaign.

Faith Murphy is the Senior Director of Sales at Oath. She leads multiple teams that focus on SMB advertising products and services.

RESOURCE
Oath: https://www.oath.com/

HACK 61

HOW TO CREATE A BLOG FOR YOUR WEBSITE

Y OUR SMALL BUSINESS needs more of an online presence than just having a basic website. To build authority in your industry, rank higher in the search engines, tell the story of your business, and build connections with current and potential customers, you need to have a blog on your site.

Blogs can also boost sales. Studies have shown most businesses that blogged at least once a month acquired customers through their blogs. And the more you blog, the more customers you can attract.

Don't freak out if you don't have the time or staff to blog every day. You can increase your web traffic without spending a lot of time or money.

Follow these steps.

1—Set goals. Before you begin, establish your goals for the blog. How will you integrate it into your overall marketing strategy? What do you hope to gain from your blog? Is it to raise brand awareness, get leads, build a community or become an industry expert. (For more on that, see Hack #21.)

2—Do your homework. You need to research other blogs in your industry. A simple search engine search will help you find the ones you're not already familiar with. If your industry is already crowded with blogs, look for an industry niche.

3—Set up the blog. To get the best results, you blog should be part of your website. There are various blogging platforms, but WordPress is the most popular one. Its simple format and many available plug-ins make it easy to set up a blog—without knowing a lot about technology.

4—Start writing. Remember, your goal is not to start a blogging business or become a writer. For you, blogging is all about marketing and promoting your business. Keep your posts short—aim for 350-500 words.

The easiest way to manage the blogging process is to create an editorial calendar to schedule your posts. Experts recommend planning your content about two months in advance and write several posts at once and schedule them.

5—Topics. What should you write about? You can talk about industry news and trends, seasonal events or holidays, or useful information about your field. Highlighting customers ("Customer of the Week or Month") is a popular blog feature. It's easy—just ask them five -10 questions and post the Q&A on your blog. Ask customers, vendors or industry experts about contributing a guest blog. Make sure the information is useful, interesting and valuable to your target customers so they'll return to your blog and tell their friends and colleagues about it. Add photos, since they add interest, make your blog look more professional and increase engagement.

6—Be professional. Make sure your grammar is correct, and there are no typos in your work. If you don't have the expertise on staff, ask someone you trust to edit your work. Check with your employees to see if any of them are good writers or editors. Do you have a staff person who can take charge of the blog? If you have the budget, consider hiring a freelancer to write about topics you assign. Before you post a blog, read it out loud. It's easier to hear if your words make sense, and you're more likely to spot any typos.

7—Market your blog. To optimize your blog for search engines, weave the same keywords into your post as your target audience uses when conducting a search. Also use those keywords in the title of your blog post.

Promote your blog in your email signature, on your social media sites and in your marketing materials. Add your blog posts to your LinkedIn account and Facebook page, and tweet links to your posts using relevant hashtags.

8—Engage with your customers. Encourage engagement with potential and current customers and clients. Ask questions in your posts. Some businesses allow readers to post comments, and reply to them. Others are warier, since your comment section can easily fill up with spam messages.

9—Consistency counts. For best results, it's crucial to be consistent. Make sure you publish on a regular basis. If your blog has old outdated information, that will reflect badly on your business.

RESOURCE
WordPress: https.//wordpress.com/

HACK 62

HOW TO CREATE A CONTENT MARKETING PROGRAM

IT'S TRUE—CONTENT REALLY is king and you must integrate it into your marketing strategy.

Content, such as articles, blog posts, white papers, videos and social media posts, can help your small business build brand awareness, attract qualified leads and increase sales. It can also establish—and cement— your reputation as an industry expert.

Here are some steps to help you develop a content marketing plan.

1—Define your goals. Before creating content, you should set measurable goals so you know what you're trying to achieve. You'll likely have different goals for different types of content. For instance, you might use Twitter to increase awareness of your small business among new customers, while LinkedIn posts may help you reach existing customers to sell them additional services.

2—Customize your content. Tailor content marketing to your specific audience. If you sell fun T-shirts to the teenage market, posting funny GIFs on Instagram and Snapchat would be a smart content strategy. But, if you're a business consultant, sharing thought leadership articles on LinkedIn is more effective. What social platforms, industry websites and other online venues do your target customers frequent? What common questions do they have about your type of product or service? What problems can you help them solve?

3—Vary your content. How-to content, visual content and online video are among the top content marketing trends, according to the Content Marketing Institute. You don't have to create multiple forms of content every time—try repurposing the same information in different formats. You can start by compiling your blog posts into a white paper or e-book, pull out interesting facts to share as tweets, and use statistics to create an infographic. If you have visuals, you can post them on Pinterest or Instagram.

4—Create a content marketing plan. Your plan should specify what types of content you will share, where you will share it, when/how often, and your goals for each piece. Assign responsibility for creating content. If you don't have the staff or talent in-house, look for freelance copywriters and designers at sites like Upwork or Freelancer. If you're going to do it yourself, Canva is a great resource for creating infographics, charts and other visuals.

5—Optimize for mobile. Whether you sell to consumers or businesses, people are looking at email, social media and websites on their mobile devices. Every piece of your content must be readable on smartphones and tablets.

6—Include a call-to-action. You cannot achieve the goals you set in Step 1 if you don't include a clear call-to-action (CTA) with each piece of content you post. Your CTA might be, "Call for an instant price quote," "Download our white paper on [X]," or "Learn more about [X]." Each CTA should link to a relevant (and mobile-friendly) landing page where viewers can take the next step, such as provide their contact information, make a purchase or fill out a form.

7—Share your content. Of course, you should post your content on your own website. But sharing it on social media is the key. If you can, budget for some social media advertising to make your content stand out in viewers' crowded feeds. Hootsuite, Buffer, and Sprout Social are popular tools to help you manage content on social media. And don't ignore email. A recent Content Marketing Institute study of B2B marketers ranked email as the most effective channel for content marketing.

8—Measure results. With digital content marketing, you can see exactly how every piece of content performs. Use social media analytics and web analytics tools to track how many people interact with each piece of content and what they do afterwards. Also test different elements (headlines, images, keywords etc.) to see which get the best response from your audience.

It's going to take some time, effort and investment, but content marketing can pay off in many ways for your small business.

RESOURCES

Content marketing trends: http://contentmarketinginstitute.com/2016/08/content-marketing-trends/

Upwork: https://www.upwork.com/

Freelancer.com: https://www.freelancer.com/

Canva: https://www.canva.com/

Content marketing research report: http://contentmarketinginstitute.com/2016/09/content-marketing-research-b2b/

HACK 63

HOW TO SET UP AFFILIATE MARKETING FOR YOUR BUSINESS

By Angel Djambazov, Cofounder, Lab6 Media

IMAGINE HAVING A NATIONAL salesforce of websites and apps, podcasters and bloggers, promoting your product, and being able to leverage them to promote your offer worldwide. Affiliate marketing provides the means to build such a team, even on a shoestring budget.

Small business owners have a wide variety of marketing options online. Some of those options may be better at driving volume, others better at developing brand awareness, but none will drive a higher Return on Ad Spend (ROAS) than affiliate marketing.

For every dollar you invest in building an affiliate program, you should get the biggest bang for your buck. Why? With most digital advertising you pay in advance, or pay on the click or impression. In affiliate marketing, you only pay affiliates when they achieve a goal you've set for them. Usually that goal is a sale or a lead.

For example, let's say you are the owner of a specialty clothing company that sells hoodies and accessories for runners. The average hoodie on your site sells for $49.99. You could promote your products on Google AdWords, which would create a lot of volume for you, but at significant financial risk. Instead, you could decide to recruit affiliates and pay them 8% commission for every sale they refer. The benefit is obvious; you control the payout and only pay those partners that perform.

If your website has a shopping cart, you can launch this type of affiliate program. That's true whether you are selling high-end furniture, collectibles, music, or even gourmet hot sauce.

More than just selling physical goods, you can also use affiliate marketing to drive leads. For instance, you might have a software company that wants customers to register for a 30-day free trial. You could setup a program that pays affiliates for every valid lead they send you.

How much to pay affiliates?

Before you set a commission rate you should:

» See if your competitors have an affiliate program and what they're paying out

» See what larger companies with similar products are paying out

» Set the payment at a level you can afford

Remember, it's much easier to start low and leverage your extra margin as a negotiating tool with your highest performing affiliates than it is to set your payout too high and try to reduce payouts after the fact.

Network or software affiliates

If your business is regional or if you're on a shoestring budget, then an affiliate software solution is right for you. This program is the least expensive, and great for regional markets. The downside is it's harder to recruit affiliates. Working with a business directly rather than through a network is a riskier proposition for affiliates. Networks provide some level of assurance to affiliates that they will get paid.

If your business is national or if you want to hit aggressive sales goals, then an affiliate network is right for you. Recruiting on networks is easier because they have large pools of affiliates that already work with other advertisers.

There is a bit more startup time required to launch with a network. You will need to install the network's tracking code on your cart or form. Networks can cost more since they take a small cut of the payout to affiliates (this is from your pocket not the affiliate's) and they may have setup fees.

Currently, the two affiliate networks friendliest to small advertisers are AvantLink and ShareASale.

WHAT DO YOUR AFFILIATES CARE ABOUT?

In general, the more lucrative a payout, the more motivated an affiliate. However, commissions aren't everything. Smart affiliates will care whether your product or service is a fit for their audience. However, your conversion rate (i.e. what percentage of visitors that they send you either purchase or sign-up) is even more critical to them. After all, you could offer them a $1,000 a sale, but if your website never converts, then all they're doing is sending you free traffic.

Affiliates will also want:

» Advertising collateral that looks professional

» Samples of your product

» Regular communication and responses to their queries

» On-time commission checks

Is affiliate marketing right for you?

No.

» You're focused on volume rather than ROAS

» You want something you can set-and-forget

» You're expecting a "get-rich-quick" solution

Yes.

» You want to work with a wide variety of sites

» You have a product or service whose value to consumers is not solely based on price

» You are focused on getting the highest return for your dollar

Angel Djambazov is the cofounder of boutique digital marketing agency Lab6 Media. He's won numerous awards, including the Affiliate Manager of the Year, Affiliate Advocate of the Year and Agency of the Year.

RESOURCES

Lab6 Media: https://lab6media.com/

AvantLink: http://www.avantlink.com/

ShareASale: https://www.shareasale.com/

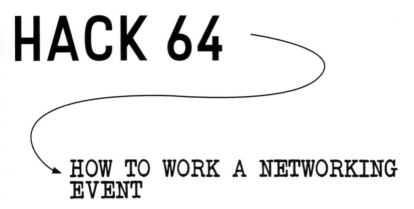

HACK 64

HOW TO WORK A NETWORKING EVENT

By Gelie Ahkenblit, CEO & Founder, NetworkingPhoenix.com

BUILDING YOUR BUSINESS through networking can be tricky. Attending events can be time consuming, following up can fall through the cracks, and no one wants to get sold to when meeting others for the first time. However, when done properly, your network could be one of your best referral sources. Nothing beats a third-party referral and word-of-mouth advertising. But simply attending events and handing out your business card to people is not the way to build a network.

Here are my top five recommendations for business networking and creating mutually beneficial relationships.

1—There is a big difference between promoting and networking. Going to an event to hand out business cards and talk about your business is promoting. Going to an event to meet interesting individuals who you can form an alliance with is networking. The easiest way to know you found someone you can build a relationship with is to ask yourself if you like this person. You are only going to do business with someone you know, like and trust—so if you are not clicking with someone—it's OK. Just move on. There are plenty of like-minded people out there who you'll have natural chemistry with and build a successful relationship.

2—No one cares about your business until they care about YOU. It's true. No one is going to do business with your business card, and no one is going to pick you over your competitor until you give them a reason to. A great way to get people on your side is to show them you are valuable. Offer them introductions, help them with a project, give them something that will create value. When people see you are willing to go the extra mile for their business and friendship, they will respond and reciprocate the favors. Once you, as the business owner, grasp this concept, your network will flourish!

3—All events are not made equal. The best way to know which event is going to be the best for you is to try them out. Unfortunately, there is no magic 8-ball to tell you if you're going to meet someone at event X or event Y. Morning events typically have a different format than evening events, and will generally attract a different type of attendees. Try events with various formats during different times of the day, and see which ones match your personality the best. That's where you are going to make the most connections.

4—Arrive early and stay late. Once you find events you'd like to try out, make sure to arrive early so you can meet the organizers, which also allows you to meet other attendees as they come in. It's much easier to strike up conversations when you're not the one having to approach people to break the ice. Staying late is also a smart idea because by the end of the event, people let their guards down, and are ready to have real conversations as opposed to "sell, sell, sell."

5—Keep it real. Unless you are being real and getting to know people on a personal level, your network will stay at a standstill. When you can find commonality with someone—such as you went to the same school, used to live in the same city, have another friend in common—you are much more likely to truly connect with that person. Once you have a personal connection, you can meet for coffee or lunch, and continue to build a mutually beneficial professional relationship.

And this goes without saying, but follow up is key. If you do all the work, but fail to follow through, you will lose the connection. Generally speaking, you have three business days to follow up with someone before the connection starts to fade. Ideally, you'll follow up with the people you're really interested immediately. Stand out by showing them that you are serious with your sense of urgency.

Gelie Akhenblit, CEO and Founder of NetworkingPhoenix.com, is an entrepreneur, speaker, mother and mentor who has altered the landscape of local networking by creating and implementing her unique online platform. NetworkingPhoenix is a huge success in the local Arizona market. Gelie is working on scaling nationally.

RESOURCE

NetworkingPhoenix: https://www.networkingphoenix.com/

HACK 65

HOW TO GET THE MOST OUT OF TRADE SHOWS

ALTHOUGH TRADE SHOWS are a big investment of time, money and effort, they're well worth attending—and exhibiting at. Trade shows have multiple purposes. Sure, they're a great place to show off your wares to potential buyers. But they're also a great place to find potential partners and suppliers, to check out your competition and to build awareness of your brand to industry media.

How do you make the most of attending a trade show? Try these tips.

1—Set measurable goals. Do you want to come home with X number of sales leads? Meet X potential partners? Close X actual deals? Defining goals helps you select the right event.

2—Choose wisely. Before committing to a show, make sure the attendees are the types of prospects you're looking for. The promoters should provide the expected number of attendees, as well as specific demographics. For example, an event for businesswomen might attract women business owners, or women who are corporate employees. You need to make sure most attendees are squarely in your target market.

3—Do advance prep. As I said, a trade show is a great place to network with people in your industry. Get a copy of the agenda and list of exhibitors as soon as possible. Study these documents to learn who is exhibiting, speaking and leading breakout sessions. Figure out who you want to connect with at the trade show, and contact them in advance (whether via phone, email or social media) to set up a meeting.

4—It's all about that booth. Look at the trade show layout online and select a booth near the entrance so attendees will still be fresh and energized when they walk by. Instead of blocking your booth entrance with a long table, put tables in the back and make the booth a welcoming space where visitors can sit down to talk. (Who doesn't welcome a chance to rest their feet at a trade show?) If those locations are already booked, look for other places most people are sure to pass by. Booths by food or beverage stations generally attract lots of people.

5—Don't be cheap. Chances are you will have to pay more for adding some "extras" to your booth. Some may not be worth the money, but I recommend opting for some cushy carpet—standing on a hard cement floor for hours is likely to sap some of your energy and productivity—and Wi-Fi. That doesn't mean you should be looking at your phone, instead of talking to show attendees, but you might want to show someone your website, some additional merchandise in your product line or pictures of your store.

6—Give and take. Bring marketing materials (brochures and business cards) to hand out, but also take visitors' contact info. You can hold a business card drawing or asking visitors to share their names and email addresses in return for information. Trade shows are an excellent opportunity to build an effective email list.

7—Network everywhere, all the time. Don't be pushy—be friendly. The person you meet on the escalator could be your next big customer. People at trade shows expect to be talked to, so don't be afraid to start a conversation.

8—Follow up. Within two weeks after the show, reach out to everyone you met to move the relationship ahead. Invite them to connect on LinkedIn, plan a lunch meeting or share some info about your business—whatever it takes to build on the connections you established at the show.

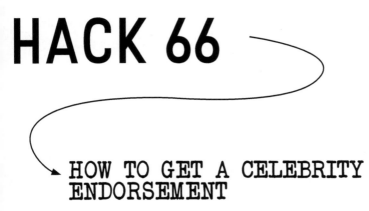

HACK 66

HOW TO GET A CELEBRITY ENDORSEMENT

By Sarah Shaw, Fashion Entrepreneur, Product Designer & Business Coach

BEFORE YOU CAN SEND anything to a celebrity, you first have to find out which celebrities appeal to your target market.

This involves four steps.

1—Defining your ideal customer. Before you can sell anything, you must first define who you're selling it to by using a Customer Profile Worksheet. Write this through the eyes of your customer, not yourself. This is perhaps the biggest mistake small business owners make in their marketing. You are not your customer. What appeals to you doesn't necessarily appeal to them.

Ultimately, what we want to know is this. Which celebrities embody the qualities your Ideal Customer aspires to? Because what a person sees on a celebrity, she often wants to buy for themselves.

2—Finding celebrities who match your ideal customer. The Customer Profile Worksheet tells you who your ideal customer is. Now you need to find out which celebrities they're drawn to. Learn as much as you can about celebrities using Google.

Successfully pitching a celebrity is all about framing your product so it appeals to what they love or care about most. While the celebrities may be hard to reach, finding out what they like is remarkably easy.

Some of your search topics might include.

» "Celebrity breast cancer survivors"
» "Celebrity pediatric cancer"
» "Celebrity cancer advocates"

Pick out the celebrities your market admires and responds to. Write down any relevant details about each of these people, such as.

» If the celebrity—or anyone they know—has been personally affected by this issue
» If they contribute to any charities or organizations related to this cause
» If they speak at or attend events related to this cause
» If the cause has an associated color, do they often wear it? Is it one of their "it" colors? (i.e. pink for breast cancer research).

3—Find the gatekeepers. The best access points are the two primary gatekeepers. managers and publicists. Their job isn't just to keep people out. It's to make sure only the *right* people get let in.

It starts with a simple website, ContactAnyCelebrity.com. This wonderful, little site has been my secret sauce for years. This site will give you the full contact information for any celebrity and their gatekeepers.

Once you find the gatekeeper, you should.

Step 1. Send your pitch email. The first step to connecting with a gatekeeper is to create a short pitch email about your product and most important, *why* the celebrity would want to have it. Basically, you are asking their permission to send the celebrity gift to their offices. It's important to keep this email short and sweet. It's always better to make your email standout from all the bland emails the gatekeepers usually get, so add your logo or some fancy images, if you can. Be sure to offer direct links to the product/s you are offering to the celebrity inside the body of the email.

Step 2. If you don't get a response, send them a quick follow up email the next day.

Step 3. Follow up. If you don't get a response to your pitch email, follow up with a phone call to the gatekeeper two days later.

4—Contact the gatekeeper after the package has been sent

1. Always track the package so you know where it is at all times.

2. Send an email to the gatekeeper.

» Three days after the package was received, follow up by email with the gatekeeper you befriended, and see if they've given it to the celebrity.

» Ask if they had a chance to open their gift from you (if you gave them one).

» If they have not given it to them yet, then ask when they might get the package to the "celebrity".

» Keep the tone super light and friendly.

3. No response? If you don't hear back, then call them two days later and ask the same questions when they answer. If they don't answer, leave one very brief message, and ask if they got your email from the specified date following up about the package you sent for the "celebrity".

4. No response again? Then keep calling every day until they answer, but only leave two messages a week.

5. Did they get it? Once you reach them, and they tell you when the celebrity will actually receive the gift, double back to them via email a week after it was to be delivered, and make sure it was received by the celebrity.

6. Yay, they got it! Once you know they "got it", the next step is to promote your new-found celebrity fan as quickly as possible. Send the good news to the media, post it on your website, and let all your stores and on-line shoppers know immediately.

Sarah Shaw is a fashion entrepreneur, product designer, and business coach. With her 20 years of experience—and six companies under her bel— Sarah has built a treasure trove of secrets for launching your line, getting your products into boutiques, to A-List celebrities, and getting massive publicity in order to grow her companies quickly.

HACK 67

HOW TO GET YOUR PRODUCT OR COMPANY ON TV

By Scott Jordan, CEO, SCOTTeVEST

A DOZEN YEARS BEFORE MY COMPANY, SCOTTeVest, appeared on *Shark Tank*, I thought I already knew everything about how to make my brand succeed.

» I knew I needed PR (and I was right).

» I also knew that I needed to hire a PR agency (and I was DEAD wrong).

Fifteen years and more than 10,000 media mentions later, I can attest that PR is indeed one of the most powerful things an entrepreneur can pursue for their business.

If you want to win as an entrepreneur, doing your own PR is essential. No one will ever be as passionate about your company as you are, and that's OK. If you are excited about what your company is doing, who better than you to get others excited?

Over the years, my company has been in every type of media out there. newspapers, TV, magazines, websites, books, tourist guides—you name it. And from my experience, TV is the pinnacle of PR. Nothing is better than getting in front of a ton of eyeballs at once and getting them excited about your company.

But, it's not easy! Here are some tips and tricks I've learned along the way.

PUT YOURSELF IN THEIR SHOES

Keep in mind that media professionals receive literally hundreds, if not thousands, of emails a day. So, any foot you can get in the door is a leg up on everyone else flooding producers' inboxes.

When pitching any media member, especially TV producers, you need to see your company or product through the producer's eyes. Don't use fluff and wild claims about your product. Get right to the point in the very first sentence about any or all of these points.

» Why should they (or anyone) care?

» What is the news angle?

» What national trends does this impact?

» What does your product/service do differently than existing solutions?

» How does this affect their audience?

The more you realize the person on the other end of the phone or computer screen is a human being, the more successful you will be at building a relationship. Also, recognize that there are two types of TV. promotional and news. Promotional covers deals, discounts and product roundups. News covers, well…news. Do *not* pitch a promotional story to news reporters as all you will receive is eye rolls, or worse—a blacklisted email address.

USE ANY CONNECTIONS YOU CAN

Leverage your network to get connected with TV producers. Post a call to action on your social channels asking if anyone has TV contacts, ask friends—ask *anyone* you know. You may be surprised with the results.

My company had occasionally worked with a freelance PR agent who had worked with some people involved with *Shark Tank*. We certainly did not get preferential treatment, but we did get two things. the email address of someone at the production company to CC on our application, and an assurance that my application would at least be seen by one person and not lost in the shuffle.

Sometimes, that's all you can get.

PERSISTENCE PAYS OFF

How many times have you heard the phrase, "the squeaky wheel gets the grease?" I firmly believe being the squeaky wheel can get most people what they want out of business and life.

Any time you don't get a hard no from the media, it could be a yes. Actually, sometimes no still means yes if you persist long enough.

How do you get your company on TV? Embrace being the squeaky wheel. If you send a press release, follow up with an email a few days later. If you send a sample, reach out when you get the delivery notification.

If someone covers you once, let them know the next time you launch a new product, then the next, then the time after that.

You don't need to be obnoxious, but you do need to get noticed and develop relationships with media members. An important part about following up is to actually progress the conversation. Don't ask, "Did you get the sample I sent?" Ask, "I saw you received the product, how do you like it so far?" Journalists don't have time to reply to emails to confirm receipt, nor do you have time to send pointless emails.

MAKE SURE YOU ARE READY

A great placement on TV *can* move a lot of product. It's not guaranteed to, but the right TV placement can liquidate your inventory very quickly. Before the segment runs, make sure you are ready for the influx of sales and traffic.

If you run out of product, that is OK. Just make sure you have a landing page or popup ready to turn on in order to take back-orders. If you don't have everything ready, your potential customers will be pissed and the TV producer won't be much happier.

DON'T RELY ON PR FOR SALES

Pursue PR in an effort to get information to the customer, but don't count on a direct correlation to sales. It's true that one single TV feature or mention *can* put you on the map, but you can't predict which one it will be, which means you can't rely on it having the effect you want and need.

SCOTTeVEST was on *The Today Show* four times before they mentioned our website address. You might think it could be a slam dunk even without the URL making it to air, but it resulted in exactly ZERO traffic. While telling your customers you were on *The Today Show* is cool, it doesn't accomplish the primary goal of PR. to get you in front of people who don't already know who you are.

PR can give you a great boost when it works, but you can never predict what will work or how well. If you are working with a PR agency, their job ends at the placement, regardless of whether it achieves the end result you need or not. To them, the outcome is out of their hands.

What they consider to be a massive victory may only be the starting gate for actual success in your business, which is usually measured in sales. When you do your own PR, you have a much more realistic, grounded and business-minded measure of what effective PR looks like, and that lets you target those opportunities and avoid wasting time on others— even if they sound good.

Scott E. Jordan is the CEO and co-founder of SCOTTeVEST, the world leader in multi-pocket clothing. He started the business from his guest bedroom with his wife Laura in 2000, and has since grown the company into one of Inc.com's fastest-growing companies, now offering more than 60 garments for men and women.

Resources

SCOTTeVest: https://www.scottevest.com/

SCOTTeVest on *The Today Show*: https://www.youtube.com/watch?v=N-40q9Epm5E

PRODUCT HACKS

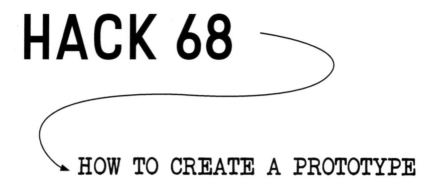

HACK 68

HOW TO CREATE A PROTOTYPE

By Keith Schacht, CEO, Mystery Science

THERE ARE FOUR KEY STEPS to building a product prototype. I use the same process whether I was working independently, working in a well-funded startup, or while working for Facebook as a product manager. Most of those prototypes turned out to be bad ideas, but about 10 were launched and developed into products, and a few went on to generate millions of dollars in sales.

1—Understand that "prototype" is plural. Never plan to build a single prototype, plan to build *many* prototypes. Prototyping is an iterative process. The first prototype you build should be ugly, it should not work, and it should look nothing like the final product you are imagining. Only after five, 10 or 15 prototypes will your prototype work, and start to resemble a final product.

2—Use verbal prototypes to test your assumptions. You assume there are many people who will want to use your product. Who are these people? In what situations will they want to use it? What do they currently use instead? What do they like and dislike about their current solution? You are making a lot of assumptions about your customers and you need to validate each one. Call people who you think will want your product and ask them 20-40 minutes of questions.

For example, if you had the idea for Uber, call people who take cabs and ask. "Do you take cabs? How often? In what situations do you choose to take a cab? Why? What do you like about the cab experience? Is there anything you dislike? Why? What if you could request a cab from your smartphone, would you like that? What if it was just a regular car and driver rather than a cab and professional driver?"

Halfway through the call, describe your idea in a few sentences and then ask "Is this something you might use? Why do you say that?" Whatever answer they give you, don't trust it. Many people will tell you they love the idea and would absolutely use it, but they are very often wrong. The same is true in reverse. People are bad at imagining a product that doesn't exist and projecting how they will react to it. The purpose of this phone call is not to understand what they think of your product idea, it's to understand your customer and how they feel about the problem you want to solve.

3—Build a really ugly, low fidelity prototype. Once you have validated your understanding of the customer, you are ready to get feedback about your idea. What parts of your product do people have the hardest time understanding as you described it over the phone? These are the parts you need to prototype. The first things you build should be rough and ugly. Its only purpose is to help you have more detailed conversations.

For a website or mobile app, simply sketch a few screens of the interface. You don't have to be good at drawing, you just need boxes and simple text labels. For a physical product such as a kitchen gadget, you could cut up existing kitchen tools and hot-glue them together. For a service you want to provide, you could role play the key interaction in your living room.

As this process evolves and you gain confidence in your product idea, increase the level of detail and start to make parts of the product work. Push the limits of your skills before hiring a professional.

4—Hire an expert to make a functioning prototype. You will eventually get beyond your skill level and need to hire an expert to make a more functional prototype. If you've built a series of rough prototypes, this stage of the process is much easier. Rather than explaining your idea abstractly, you're showing them the same rough versions you validated with customers. This person will do a better job building what you want, and can more easily estimate how much their services will cost. For digital prototypes, Crew.co and Upwork.com are two websites for finding professionals. For physical prototypes, you can find an industrial design consultant by contacting IDSA.org. To save money, your local college likely has computer science students and industrial design students.

The key to this entire process is understanding that the goal is not to build a prototype, it's to understand your customers and validate your idea. Prototypes are simply a tool for learning, and building a functioning prototype comes after you've validated the needs of your customer.

Keith Schacht is the CEO of Mystery Science, a science education company based in San Francisco.

RESOURCE

Mystery Science: *http://mysteryscience.com*

HACK 69

HOW TO MANUFACTURE PRODUCTS OVERSEAS

By Nichole Rairigh, Founder & CEO, The Apparel Agency

THERE ARE FIVE IMPORTANT steps for manufacturing your product overseas that start with identifying manufacturers that meet your needs and end with receiving shipment of the final product.

1—Find manufacturers by asking for referrals and attending industry trade shows. Start your search for an overseas manufacturer by asking other businesses in your industry for referrals. Who do they use to manufacture their product? Are they satisfied? How did they come across this manufacturer and why did they decide to go with them? Be mindful these businesses won't share this information with you if they're a competitor.

Another good place to find overseas manufacturers is at industry trade shows. Within every industry, there are tradeshows where manufacturers present their capabilities for various good and services. Off-shore manufacturers that are government funded will often attend these trade shows because they are trying to promote their economies and businesses in their area. Often, the trade show will have designated areas for different regions. These are great places to talk to manufacturing representatives who live in that area, or have sourcing agents in that area, who can align you with the right manufacturer.

Materials suppliers may also have leads with manufacturers they can refer. For example, the apparel industry has sourcing trade shows where you can find fabric suppliers that can give great referrals for manufacturers that work with specific types of fabric. Just ask!

Manufacturers each have different capabilities, skill levels, and types of machinery. Machines are run a specific way for each specific type of product. Uniforms are manufactured differently than dresses, for example. Evaluate your needs and narrow your search to manufacturers that match those needs.

2—Meet with manufacturers and evaluate samples. Once you locate manufacturers that seem to match your needs, you need to see product samples. Overseas manufacturers wanting to start a relationship will often travel to you, bringing examples of their work called "quality samples". If they don't travel to you in person, they will at the very least send quality samples.

With a domestic manufacturer, you have the ability to be on-site and hold them accountable. Offshore manufacturers, on the other hand, are only as good as the packages you receive. You will get a good feel for the company based on the quality of these samples. In the apparel industry, we get a good feel for quality, construction and fits. We also have an idea of what we're getting based on the region we're getting it from. Vietnam, Cambodia, and Bangladesh are go-to regions for cheap, fast fashion whereas fine-needle, high-quality work is a better coming from Europe and China.

In addition to sample quality, evaluate the manufacturer's capacity, types of machinery and equipment, and their pricing. If you're a new business, there may be manufacturers willing to service you while you are small, and meet the demands of small batch manufacturing, but a lot of bigger manufacturing companies won't.

3—Choose a manufacturer who aligns with your needs. Align yourself with the manufacturer who has the equipment and proximity of materials that meet your needs. Discuss minimums, payment structure, and the ability and capacity of the manufacturer to meet your demands. You'll also want to consider the import taxes and customs the United States will impose for doing business overseas, as this will add to your overall costs, and may be one of the deciding factors for which country you choose to manufacture in.

There is a higher level of risk with overseas manufacturers than there is with onshore manufacturers. With offshore manufacturers, you order "full package". If they find comparable fabric that's less expensive to source, they make that final call. They sew it, cut it, and deliver it, and you may wonder—why doesn't this stretch the way my sample does? Why is the shade a little different? The amount of risk you are willing to take is a good indicator of whether you should manufacture domestically or offshore.

That being said, also remember as much as you're leery of offshore manufacturers, they're also leery of you. Unless you are working with a con artist, they're there to deliver—that's how they stay in business. It is a partnership; they need your business and you need theirs.

4—Develop the product and evaluate the manufacturer. The development phase is not the same as production. Production is when you're running thousands of units on the developed product. The development phase is where you work out all the kinks, and make sure the manufacturer can produce the quality of product you're happy with before they produce thousands of units. This may take several iterations.

Use the development phase as another layer of vetting. Just because a manufacturer met the front-end requirements discussed above, doesn't mean they will meet the other requirements necessary to be the right manufacturer for you. Assess whether they're going to be able to meet your demands, or are they just sending you inadequate results?

Small business owners must have the patience and finances to be able to go through the development process and vet the manufacturer even further.

5—Produce and evaluate the final product. The production process is yet another layer of vetting manufacturers. Evaluate the following.

Was everything to order? Were there any issues with receiving? With quality? With pricing? With packaging?

Just because you did your first round of production with this manufacturer, doesn't mean you have to continue working with them. You want a manufacturing partner that passes all the tests, from capabilities to samples to development to production and delivering the final product.

Mistakes do happen. It's always possible something happens outside of your control, and you don't learn about it until the end. Do your best to vet and evaluate along the way.

Nichole Rairigh is the founder and CEO of The Apparel Agency, an apparel development and production management agency that provides solutions to brands worldwide.

RESOURCE

The Apparel Agency: http://www.theapparelagency.com/

HACK 70

HOW TO FIND A DOMESTIC MANUFACTURING SITE

BY NICHOLE RAIRIGH, FOUNDER & CEO, THE APPAREL AGENCY

HERE ARE FIVE CONSIDERATIONS for finding the right domestic manufacturing site for your business.

1—Be willing to pay more. Domestic manufacturing is more expensive than manufacturing overseas because labor costs in the United States are high compared to other countries. The United States is all about higher education, therefore it's difficult to find skilled labor. No one goes to college to become a seamstress. However, even though it's more expensive, there are major benefits to manufacturing in the United States versus overseas that can justify the higher labor costs.

2—Know the benefits of domestic manufacturing. The main benefit of working with domestic manufacturers is being able to manage the process more closely than you would be able to if the manufacturing site were across the world. You can visit the site, get your hands on the product, and work directly with the owner of the machines who is also going to be assembling your product. With overseas manufacturers, this often isn't the case, as you're more likely to be working with managers and representatives of the manufacturing company. Offshore production is out of your hands, whereas domestic manufacturing allows you to have a much more intimate experience with your product. A lot of the time it makes more sense to work domestically to develop your products. Because you're able to manage the process more closely, there is less risk, and you can ensure the product is produced to your standards.

3—Ask for referrals and utilize community RESOURCES. Start with a simple internet search to familiarize yourself with what types of manufacturers are out there. It is much easier to find domestic manufacturers online than it is overseas manufacturers.

Check with your city to see if there are any business directories you can tap into to find local manufacturers. Local small business development centers and associations can also give you referrals and help you get started on the right track.

Be sure to ask other businesses in your industry for referrals as well. Who do they use to manufacture their product? Are they satisfied? How did they come across this manufacturer, and why did they decide to go with them? These businesses won't share this information with you if they're a competitor.

Also, be creative. I tapped into a state-funded fashion program to find my manufacturers. I got the name of one person, and that one person gave me three other people to talk to, and it spiraled from there.

4—Be a student of the manufacturing process. It's critical to know the process of manufacturing. Understand you're not going to go in there and tell the manufacturer how to manufacture your product. Be a student first—learn how the industry works—and be willing to accept that. There is a misconception that the development process—the part of the manufacturing process where you work out all the kinks—should be free in order to win your business. Unless you're going to promise to fill the manufacturer's capacity for the next year or two, this is not possible. And most startups can't make that promise.

Also, business owners may want to enter the manufacturing process thinking they want to run production. If this is the case, you best know what you're doing. Don't assume the manufacturer is going to pave the road for you; they're going to assume you know what you're doing or you would have hired someone to do it for you. It's important that business owners know what they know and most important, what they don't know.

5—Evaluate the manufacturers. Evaluate the manufacturer's development process and their access to vendors and suppliers. It's important to understand the manufacturer may or may not have the capabilities to develop for you. Are they equipped to spec, design, fit and get your product to a place where it's ready to sell? This is a much different and more involved process than working with a manufacturer that has ready-to-sell, private label products that are ready for your brand name to be attached. Also consider if they can accommodate the size of your production run. There may be manufacturers willing to service you while you are a small company, and meet the demands of small batch manufacturing, but a lot of bigger manufacturing companies won't.

Nichole Rairigh is the founder and CEO of The Apparel Agency, an apparel development and production management agency that provides solutions to brands worldwide.

RESOURCE
The Apparel Agency: http://www.theapparelagency.com/

HACK 71

HOW TO SELL YOUR PRODUCTS ON AMAZON

THERE ARE SEVERAL WAYS to sell your products. One smart way is to sell your products on Amazon, the country's largest marketplace. Here's how to get started.

Your first step is to decide if you're going to sell as a "professional" or an "individual". Professionals sell more than 40 items a month. At press time, that will cost you $39.99 a month, plus other fees. If you expect to sell less than 40 items, register as an individual. There is a $0.99 per sales charge, plus other fees.

Then.

1—What do you plan to sell? All sellers can choose from over 20 product categories. Professional sellers have an additional 10 product categories to choose from.

2—Register your account on Amazon's Seller Central.

3—After you register, the process is simple.

a. List your products. If your merchandise is already available on Amazon, all you have to do is indicate the number of products you're selling, the condition they're in and shipping options you're offering. If the products are not on Amazon, you need to identify the UPC/EAN and SKU numbers and add product descriptions.

Start selling. Once you've listed your merchandise, they're visible on Amazon.com. Your listings should be accurate and your photos should highlight the product. (See Hack 41 for more photo tips.)

b. Ship. You have two options. You can handle shipping yourself, or use Fulfillment by Amazon, where they ship for you (for a fee, of course).

c. Get paid. Amazon direct deposits payments into your bank account, and then notifies you a payment has been made.

Of course, Amazon is only one marketplace. There are plenty more. Alibaba wants to attract more American companies. Etsy, Walmart and eBay attract millions of shoppers.

RESOURCES

Amazon has a primer on its site. https.//services.amazon.com/selling/benefits.htm/ref=asus_soa_snav_ben_t1.

Want to know more about selling on Amazon vs. eBay, read: http://www.cpcstrategy.com/blog/2017/03/selling-on-amazon-vs-ebay/

HACK 72

HOW TO GET YOUR PRODUCT INTO A BIG BOX RETAILER

By Vicki Reece, Founder & CEO, Joy of Mom

I F YOU WANT TO GET your product in a big box retailer it can be done, but you must navigate through the obstacles.

1—How to get an appointment with a buyer of a big box store. Research who the buyer is for your product category at the store; then cold call or email them. Persistent pays off as you'll need to stay on it until they get back to you. If you don't hear from them, and you truly feel your product is right for that retailer, be resourceful through your network, and see who may know someone to make an introduction for your company.

2—Pricing products for a big box store. Do your research to see what the competition charges for their products. Be flexible so the big box buyer can help determine your products' price points. Be open to their advice on pricing—they know their stores and market and you both want to your products to sell-through.

3—Producing enough product for the initial shipment. Produce enough products for your order with a little extra, depending on your financial position. Check where the price breaks are in manufacturing. Stocking a lot of extra inventory can be expensive. Do your research to find out the most reasonable price and terms without comprising on quality, and which manufacturer fits any cash flow constraints you have.

4—Getting paid on time. Set up terms and agreements upfront. Have your attorney review all contracts. While it may be difficult for the big box retailer to change anything, at least you know what the expectations are. They may want longer terms, such as 60 or 90 days, or only pay for the products when the items sell. Know the payment schedule, and include it in the agreement so there are no surprises. If you have any issues collecting, contact your buyer or the billing office.

5—Handle returns. Only ship the initial order, and have a reserve for reorder/s that is manageable for your company's resources. Make sure you have cash in reserve if you need to take product back. Also find out what the detailed return policies are for damaged product or any unsatisfied customers.

6—How do you get them to reorder? If possible, ask for the data that can track sales by store of your product, and how fast it is turning. Find out how your buyer handles reorders.

Vicki Reece, is the founder and CEO of Joy of Mom.

RESOURCE
Joy of Mom: http://joyofmom.com/

HACK 73

HOW TO SET THE PERFECT INVENTORY LEVEL

O NE OF THE KEY METRICS in running a successful company is maintaining the correct level of inventory. This is a tricky proposition because in this now "on-demand" economy, customers always want their product "ASAP". For most goods, delivery of anything that takes more than two days is typically unacceptable to the needs of the customer. This means you most likely must have your products in stock so they can be shipped the same day. However, keeping all the products that customers want in inventory is an expensive investment.

Money spent on stocking inventory eats up cash flow that could otherwise be used to grow the business or be taken as profit by the owner. Your goal is to achieve the perfect balance between customer satisfaction and cash inventory investment.

Here is how to do it.

1—Watch the turns. You need to know how many times per year or month your inventory turns. This means how often is a product out of stock, and replaced by a new purchase order as a result of customer orders. A higher number of turns is good for the business, since it shows products are being sold and are not stuck in inventory, using cash. You should know the turns for the inventory as a whole, plus for each individual product. The exact turn number will vary by industry, and should be compared to how the company has done in past years. However, a lower turn number always uses more cash flow than a higher turn one.

2—Calculate the fulfillment rate. This is the percentage of times a customer orders a product that is actually in stock. The correct fulfillment rate will vary by company. A higher rate is obviously better, but requires more cash flow to maintain since more inventory needs to be on hand. The best rate is one that keeps customers satisfied, and not have them cancel the order. This is about correctly setting their expectations for when they will receive their products.

3—Set the ROPs and ROQs. A critical metric in keeping inventory turns high is to determine for each product the reorder point (ROP) and reorder quantity (ROQ). The ROP is how many units are in stock at the time the product is repurchased for inventory. The ROQ is how many units are ordered at the time of repurchase from the supplier. Getting both numbers right is critical to managing cash flow and customer satisfaction.

When setting the ROP, consider transit time to receive new products for inventory and how many of them are sold per day. Setting the ROP low will save cash, but may decrease the fulfillment rate and customer satisfaction. Setting the ROP too high, will needlessly use cash through a high inventory level. When setting the ROQ, also determine the rate of sale and if there are special vendor discounts for ordering higher quantities of that product. Setting the ROQ too low may result in ordering too frequently, and increased shipping charges. Setting it too high will increase the use of cash and therefore, lower inventory turns.

4—Leverage dropships. A lower inventory may be able to be maintained if you can dropship directly from your suppliers. The advantage is you don't have to worry about taking products from inventory, and your cash flow is unaffected. Unfortunately, many suppliers will not ship single orders to customers, but, don't give up. The downside of dropshipping is you give up the name of your customer to your supplier, who may also be a competitor.

You also lose control of the process in getting the product to the customer, and how it arrives. With dropships, the supplier may require immediate payment of their invoice (instead of when it is sent in quantity for inventory), which may negate any cash flow savings.

Doing inventory management well requires data analysis and practice for any company. Test, order more product, and repeat to find the turns, fulfillment rate, ROP and ROQ that are appropriate to run your company.

HR HACKS

HACK 74

HOW TO KNOW THE RIGHT TIME TO HIRE YOUR FIRST EMPLOYEE

I F YOU'RE SERIOUS ABOUT growing your small business, at some point you're going to need to hire someone to help you. How do you know when you should take the giant step of becoming an employer? Ask yourself these four questions.

1—Are you busy enough to justify hiring someone? Is your cash flowing regularly or do you have seasonal peaks and valleys? You shouldn't hire a permanent employee until you have enough steady work to keep him or her busy even during slow times.

If you're not quite at that point yet, opt for hiring temporary workers, outsourcing to independent contractors, or hiring part-time employees or interns instead.

But, if business is consistently booming—if you've had to actually turn away work, for instance—then chances are you're ready to hire a full-time employee. Also, make sure the steady work is something you're willing to delegate and can train someone else to do.

2—Do you no longer have the skill set needed to grow your business? Entrepreneurs, especially during the startup stage, have to be jacks-of-all-trades. But as you grow, it gets harder to focus on all aspects of your business and give them the attention they need.

3—Are you financially ready for hiring your first employee? Hiring your first employee isn't cheap. First, there's the cost of advertising the position, possibly running background checks, and the cost of the time spent reviewing resumes and interviewing candidates.

Once the employee comes onboard, their hourly wages aren't the only expense you have to deal with. You may need to buy new equipment for the person, like a computer and workstation. You'll also have to pay social security taxes, Medicare taxes, payroll taxes and state unemployment taxes. If you plan to offer employee benefits, such as health insurance or a 401(k) plan, know that benefits can *cost 20% of the employee's wages* or more. Finally, you may need to buy workers' compensation insurance.

Your business's cash flow is a deciding factor in whether or not you're ready to hire. You've got to have enough cash in your accounts on payday to cover payroll—you can't ask employees to wait a couple extra days to get their paychecks because your customers haven't paid you yet.

4—Are you ready to deal with red tape? As soon as you start the hiring process, you have to comply with state and federal anti-discrimination employment laws when advertising the job, interviewing candidates, testing them, and making your offer. The red tape only gets more tangled once your first employee comes onboard. You *must*.

» Pay employees the minimum wage (either the federal minimum wage or one set by your state, whichever is higher)

» Maintain records of employee time worked, wages paid, and overtime.

» Follow workplace safety regulations and may be required to purchase workers' compensation insurance

» Make sure the employee benefits you offer comply with federal regulations

Hiring your first employee isn't a decision to be made lightly. By asking yourself the questions above, you can make an informed choice—one that helps grow your business.

If you determine you don't need to hire permanent workers, consider outsourcing to independent contractors. (see Hack #82). For more information about your state's and federal labor laws, see the resource listing below.

RESOURCES

How much should you pay your employees? https.//www.fundera.com/blog/how-much-should-i-pay-my-employees

Top payroll mistakes small business owners make: https.//www.fundera.com/blog/top-5-payroll-mistakes

State Labor Offices: https.//www.dol.gov/whd/contacts/state_of.htm

Federal labor laws: https.//www.dol.gov/whd/flsa/

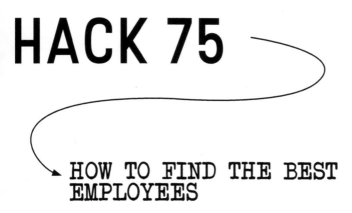

HACK 75

HOW TO FIND THE BEST EMPLOYEES

POSTING JOBS ON various sites like Craigslist or Monster can bring in a lot of unqualified people, and be a big waste of time. For most small businesses, hiring a recruiter who collects 25% of the first year's compensation is out of reach. The key is to find people who have the required skills, and the right cultural fit at a reasonable search price.

Here is the best way to do it.

1—Ask current employees. People socialize with people like them. If you want to find workers similar to your current employees, ask them for referrals. Pay a $250 to $1,000 bonus to your employees who refer a job candidate you hire, and who stays for at least 90 days.

2—Post openings on the company's website. Many candidates are doing job searches through Google and Bing. Posting job descriptions with the appropriate search keywords will get the job opening found by job seekers.

3—List the opening in every employee's email signature. Use a simple sentence and link in the signature of every outgoing email from the company. For example, "We are growing! We need sales and marketing superstars. Check out these opportunities". Then add the appropriate hyperlink for the website.

4—Search employees at competitors on LinkedIn. Find competitors who have the employees that your company is looking for. Get connected to them and see if they are interested in making a switch. Some websites even list key employees.

5—Niche job boards. Look at the smaller job boards that focus on a specific job candidate. The more niched the job board, the better the quality of applications you will receive. Or search the freelance sites, such as Guru.com or Upwork.com.

6—Ask social media. Post weekly on your social platforms any current openings. This enables your followers to spread the word as well.

7—Search trade shows or other industry events. These often have job boards. Check out who is speaking on the various panels to source higher-level positions. I once saw a company executive at a trade show wearing a button that said, "I am looking to hire you."

HACK 76

HOW TO HIRE YOUR FIRST EMPLOYEE

F YOUR BUSINESS IS BOOMING, but you are struggling to keep up, perhaps it's time to hire some help. The eight steps below, from the Small Business Administration, can help you start the hiring process and ensure you are compliant with key federal and state regulations.

STEP 1. OBTAIN AN EMPLOYER IDENTIFICATION NUMBER (EIN)

Before hiring your first employee, you need to get an employment identification number (EIN) from the U.S. Internal Revenue Service. The EIN is often referred to as an Employer Tax ID or as Form SS-4. The EIN is necessary for reporting taxes and other documents to the IRS. In addition, the EIN is necessary when reporting information about your employees to state agencies. Apply for EIN online or contact the IRS at 1-800-829-4933.

STEP 2. SET UP RECORDS FOR WITHHOLDING TAXES

According to the IRS, you must keep records of employment taxes for at least four years. Keeping good records can also help you monitor the progress of your business, prepare financial statements, identify sources of receipts, keep track of deductible expenses, prepare your tax returns, and support items reported on tax returns.

Below are three types of withholding taxes you need for your business.

» **Federal Income Tax Withholding**

Every employee must provide an employer with a signed withholding exemption certificate (Form W-4) on or before the date of employment. The employer must then submit Form W-4 to the IRS.

» **Federal Wage and Tax Statement**

Every year, employers must report to the federal government wages paid and taxes withheld for each employee. This report is filed using Form W-2, wage and tax statement. Employers must complete a W-2 form for each employee who they pay a salary, wage or other compensation.

Employers must send Copy A of W-2 forms to the Social Security Administration by the last day of February to report wages and taxes of your employees for the previous calendar year. In addition, employers should send copies of W-2 forms to their employees by Jan. 31 of the year following the reporting period.

» **State Taxes**

Depending on the state where your employees are located, you may be required to withhold state income taxes. Visit the state and local tax page for more information.

STEP 3. EMPLOYEE ELIGIBILITY VERIFICATION

Federal law requires businesses to verify an employee's eligibility to work in the United States. Within three days of hire, employers must complete Form I-9, employment eligibility verification, which requires employers to examine documents to confirm the employee's citizenship or eligibility to work in the U.S. Employers can only request documentation specified on the I-9 form.

Employers do not need to submit the I-9 form with the federal government but are required to keep them on file for three years after the date of hire or one year after the date of the employee's termination, whichever is later.

Employers can use information taken from the Form I-9 to electronically verify the employment eligibility of newly hired employees by registering with E-Verify.

STEP 4. REGISTER WITH YOUR STATE'S NEW HIRE REPORTING PROGRAM

All employers are required to report newly hired and re-hired employees to a state directory within 20 days of their hire or rehire date.

STEP 5. OBTAIN WORKERS' COMPENSATION INSURANCE

All businesses with employees are required to carry workers' compensation insurance coverage through a commercial carrier, on a self-insured basis or through their state's Workers' Compensation Insurance program.

STEP 6. POST REQUIRED NOTICES

Employers are required to display certain posters in the workplace that inform employees of their rights and employer responsibilities under labor laws.

STEP 7. FILE YOUR TAXES

Generally, employers who pay wages subject to income tax withholding, Social Security and Medicare taxes must file IRS Form 941, Employer's Quarterly Federal Tax Return.

RESOURCES

Small Business Administration: https.//www.sba.gov/

Get an Employer Identification Number (EIN): https.//www.irs.gov/businesses/small-businesses-self-employed/apply-for-an-employer-identification-number-ein-online

IRS recordkeeping rules: https.//www.irs.gov/taxtopics/tc305.html

IRS employer tax guide: https.//www.irs.gov/pub/irs-pdf/p15.pdf

IRS form W-4: https.//www.irs.gov/uac/about-form-w4

IRS form W-2: https.//www.irs.gov/uac/about-form-w2

State tax obligations: https.//www.sba.gov/starting-business/filing-paying-taxes/determine-your-state-tax-obligations

E-Verify: https.//www.uscis.gov/e-verify

New Hire reporting: https.//www.sba.gov/managing-business/running-business/human-resources/new-hire-reporting-your-state

IRS form 941: https.//www.irs.gov/uac/about-form-941

HACK 77

HOW TO INTERVIEW PROSPECTIVE EMPLOYEES

THERE ARE VARIOUS WAYS to conduct job interviews, but no matter which method you choose, there are certain questions you likely will want to ask—but be careful. There are several questions you simply cannot legally ask. While some of these may seem innocent or innocuous, asking a job candidate to answer them could potentially get you in trouble, since many are prohibited by anti-discrimination laws. A job candidate you decide not to hire—for whatever reason—might decide to sue you, claiming you discriminated against them.

So, what can you ask during a job interview?

Don't ask. "Are you a U.S. citizen?"

Instead, ask. "Are you authorized to work in the United States?" (New employees need to fill out an employment eligibility verification I-9 document—but not until they're hired.)

Don't ask. "How old are you?"

Instead, ask. If you legitimately need to know a person's age—for instance, if the job requires serving alcohol—you can ask about their legal ability to do the job. "Are you of legal age to serve alcohol?"

Don't ask. "Are there any religious holidays or hours that you can't work?"

Instead, ask. "Are you able to work all the days and hours this job requires?"

Don't ask. "Are you married?" "Do you have children?" "Are you pregnant?" "Are you planning to have children soon?"

Instead, ask. If you're concerned that the candidate will want to leave work early or be reluctant to travel on business, ask in a way that relates to the job duties. For instance, "This job requires a lot of travel; will that be a problem for you?" "This job requires working on weekends; is that a problem?" or "We frequently work overtime here; will that be a problem?"

Don't ask. "How is your health?" "Do you have any mental or physical disabilities?"

Instead, ask. "Can you perform the duties this job requires?" "Are you willing to take a drug and/or alcohol test?" It's illegal to reject a job candidate because of mental or physical disabilities, health problems or addictions.

Don't ask. "What country are you from?" "What's your ethnic background?"

Instead, ask. Actually, there is no right way to ask about race or ethnicity. The Civil Rights Act of 1964 prohibits it—so don't even ask.

Don't ask. "Have you been hospitalized in the last year?" "How many sick days did you take last year?"

Instead, ask. "Can you meet the attendance requirements of this job?"

Don't let these "rules" intimidate you. The general principle is simple. Keep your questions focused on whether the person meets the requirements of the job, and you'll be in good shape.

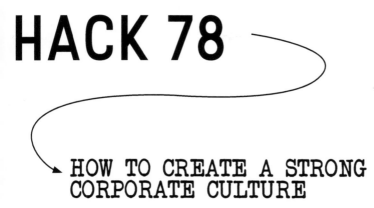

HACK 78

HOW TO CREATE A STRONG CORPORATE CULTURE

DON'T MAKE THE COMMON mistake of thinking your business is too small to worry about corporate culture. Every business—no matter its size—has a corporate culture. Though it sounds, well, corporate, a corporate culture is simply the shared values, traditions and goals that make it unique. The difference is, strong corporate cultures arise consciously, shaped by the business owner, while weak ones arise accidentally from neglect.

If you're not sure what your corporate culture is, follow these steps to help you form one.

1—Refer to your mission statement. We talked about this in Hack #1. Your mission statement is a great leaping off point developing your corporate culture.

2—Be authentic. Corporate culture should be a natural outgrowth of your business's mission, your industry, your customers and even your personality. Don't try to "force" a corporate culture that's not authentic.

3—Involve your team. Although you are a key driver of your business's corporate culture, that doesn't mean you can impose it from the top down. Involve your employees in determining what kind of culture they want to create.

4—Hire for fit. Look for job candidates whose personalities and attitudes mesh with your culture. Fit is more important than skill. A job candidate might have years of experience, but if he or she is uptight and rigid while your culture is loose and fun, the new hire won't be happy—and neither will you.

5—Spread the message. Everything from the design of your office or stores, to the appearance and tone of your marketing materials, to the way your employees interact with customers should clearly convey your corporate culture to the outside world.

6—"Culture" does not equal "crazy." Wacky corporate cultures may get a lot of attention, but is that the brand awareness you want to build? You want to project an image of being ethical and responsible to create a firm foundation for growth.

7—Be ready to change. Nothing stays static in business today, and the corporate culture that works when your company is in the early stages may need to evolve as your business grows. If your corporate culture needs a tune-up—or an overhaul—don't be afraid to make changes.

HACK 79

HOW TO SET COMPENSATION FOR YOUR STAFF

By Erica Morrison, Chief People Officer, Brandify

THE GREATEST SKILL you will learn to master in setting, communicating, and creating transparent cultures will be effectively knowing how to address compensation.

STEP 1. THE PSYCHOLOGY OF COMPENSATION

The purpose of compensation should be to *reward* your employees for their hard work and service. They will magically appear, hardwired, with a collection of talents, intellect and passion, and what you must do is reward them for selecting your company as the showcase. You must be able to justify your salary structure by identifying industry standards, experience, education or placement of business. If you avoid this step, you expose your business and reputation—beating around the bush only attempts to compensate for what's clearly lacking. Your conversations around compensation should never feel guilty, with words struggling to crawl from your mouth, but instead should feel strong, extending convincing plans and promises. Your beliefs and theories surrounding compensation will be embedded within your company culture, so let go of the guilt and pick up the power by first checking your compensation psychology.

Pro Tip. You may not be able to offer market rates—that's okay, just be honest. You might be surprised to find those entrepreneurial spirits who are willing to dream along with your mission and vision.

STEP 2. SOME RESEARCH IS WORTH IT

Some shortcuts in life are not worth taking. The same idea applies to compensation research. Here are three helpful tips to consider.

1. *Salary Guides.* There are many recruiting consulting firms that research, assemble and publish free salary guides; Robert Half, Randstad, and Payscale are just a few. In gathering your research, you should be able to get a clear picture of what the industry "standards" are.

2. *Industry Specifics.* Your employees may venture to Glassdoor, Indeed and other public forums to discover what their compensation should be—beat them to it! It is in your best interest to identify the benefits other businesses in your market are offering when it comes to compensation.

3. *Salary Metrics.* After conducting the above research translate the work into one reliable salary metric. You will be able to reference the resource to justify selected salaries. If you would like an example, remember, Google is your friend.

Pro Tip. Compensation standards are constantly evolving. Make sure to revisit these steps once a year.

STEPS 3,4 & 5. BECOMING A HORTICULTURIST OF PEOPLE

Horticulturist of People (noun). A person who tends to the science and art of cultivating people.-

When asked to illustrate, or define the operational structure of your business you may default to the "well-oiled machine" model; with your employees symbolizing the bolts that keep everything intact. However, people are not machines, they are more like plants. So, for you to cultivate a botanical garden of people (your employees) you must prioritize the following three steps.

STEP 3. OFFERING A GOOD BASE/SOIL

Compensation is the soil or base for your employees. If you initially provide the proper base, you will allow your employees to grow roots into something worth growing into.

STEP 4. NURTURING/WATERING

Not all compensation is monetary. Your employees will want to grow as they adjust into their roles. They will search for training, mentorship and additional avenues for continuous learning. Make the time to discover your team's strengths, weaknesses, opportunities and threats (S.W.O.T) in addition to their personal interests. In doing this you allow your team to grow at exponential rates, increasing the collective experience and productivity of your business.

> *Pro Tip. Utilize psychometric tests ("What color is your brain", "16 personalities", "D.I.S.C", "Emotional Intelligence", "Myers-Briggs", "Leadership Style", Visual dna- "Who am I" etc.) to discover your team's personality, the results will assist in structuring effective training. Discover your team's industry role models (preferably local) and create shadowing opportunities, or conversations in person or over the phone. If nothing else, make sure you know who your employees' role models are; who we are inspired by says a lot about who we are.*

STEP 5. EXPOSURE / SUNLIGHT

As your team continues to support your dreams make sure you do the same in supporting theirs. Achieve your goals by incentivizing your teams through their personal passions. In acknowledging their desires and passions you will never shine brighter.

Pro Tip. *Discover your employee's personal goals, this will keep you up to date on how to surprise and support them from seed to blossom.*

Before you collect your gardening tools, know that weeds may arise. You will incur the occasional bad hire and make mistakes, but keep planting. Your future garden will thank you.

Erica Morrison is currently the Chief People Officer at Brandify, an industry-leading provider of location-based digital marketing solution.

RESOURCE

Brandify: http://www.brandify.com/

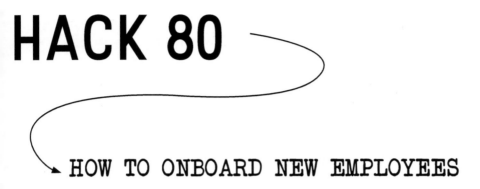

HACK 80

HOW TO ONBOARD NEW EMPLOYEES

THE PROPER ONBOARDING of new employees is nearly as important as hiring the right people for the job. Your goal is to make sure your new hires feel welcome on day one. Here's how.

1—Deal with the paperwork in advance. Spending their first day at work filling out a stack of forms does not make a new employee feel welcome. Mail your new hires their W-4 forms, I-9 employment eligibility verification forms, emergency contact information and other documents ahead of time to print out, sign and bring in on the first day. This will help them get started working on day one.

2—Send them an employee handbook. Help new hires familiarize themselves with your company by getting them a copy of your employee handbook (or employee manual). The handbook should cite your policies, including work hours, breaks, sick time and vacation time, pay schedule and dress codes. Have employees read the handbook and sign a document confirming they understand the information.

3—Prep their workspace. Prepare all the essentials, whether that's a uniform for your new server, a laptop for your new bookkeeper, or business cards for your new salesperson, so the person can get right to work. Make sure their computer—and any other equipment is ready to go.

4—Meeting the team. Introduce them to their new coworkers. If your staff is big enough that remembering names might be difficult (and on day one that's very likely), provide some type of cheat sheet or org chart to help. Along with introductions, explain what each employee does so the new staffer can get a lay of the land.

5—Create a buddy system. Have another employee in the same department serve as a buddy for the new employee during their first week or two. They can answer questions (especially questions the new worker may not want to bother their boss about, provide introductions and generally make the person feel welcome. A buddy can also be invaluable in introducing the new worker to your company culture, such as the happy hours the accounting department goes to on Fridays or the company softball team. Some companies take the buddy system one step further and create a mentor/mentee relationship that lasts for a few months.

6—Make the person feel special. Plan for you or some co-workers to take the new employee out to lunch on the first day. This not only gives everyone a chance to get to know one another better, but also makes the new employee feel special on a stressful day.

7—Job training. Assign someone to provide job training to the new hire. Set up regular check-ins, such as at the end of the first day, end of the first few weeks and the end of each month before the first 90 days, to make sure the employee is acclimating properly.

HACK 81

HOW TO GIVE BONUSES TO YOUR EMPLOYEES

THIS A VERY TRICKY THING to determine since many bonuses are not given objectively for several reasons. For many jobs (besides sales), it is difficult to base the bonus on a particular financial contribution to the company. In some cases, small business owners use bonuses as a means to exert financial control over their employees. In other cases, where bonuses are more subjective, employees think getting them are just part of the job, and they'll get one every year. Finally, some owners just give up, and give automatic holiday bonuses to everyone. This can become one big trap. Here is how to solve it.

1—Salespeople don't get bonuses, they make commission. However, they can get holiday bonuses.

2—Bonuses for other employees need to be set quarterly or bi-annually. Use specific written and measurable objectives agreed upon at the beginning of each time period. Do not leave this for later in the quarter. Many small business owners want to keep this subjective because they want "power" over the employee. Instead, create a way to give bonuses based on accomplishments that both parties can agree were achieved or not.

3—Holiday bonuses. Companies should give nominal holiday bonuses of less than $500 because employees come to expect them annually, regardless of company performance. Holiday bonuses should not be used to send a message to a particular employee. They should not be based on anything except the good cheer of being part of the company. If your business had an exceptionally good year, then the bonus amount could be increased

Instead of cash, you can also give employees gift cards or a special gift, with a thoughtful note about how important they are to your company. If possible, a company holiday party can also boost the celebration culture this time of year.

4—Recognition. What many employees want (besides cash) is recognition from you and their peers that they did a good job. Make this happen through letters, emails, or at company meetings.

HACK 82

HOW TO FIND AND MANAGE INDEPENDENT CONTRACTORS

MANY SMALL BUSINESSES couldn't survive without independent contractors. They help you do more than you could possibly accomplish on your own. Hiring freelancers enables you to save money because you don't have to offer benefits. And since you only hire by the project, you're not stuck with staff at slow times. Also, independent contractors can offer you specialized services you likely couldn't afford to hire on a full-time basis.

There are numerous independent contractor marketplaces where you can find help. A few include Fiverr, 99Designs, Upwork, Guru and Freelancer.

Managing independent contractor relationships can get tricky. Here are some tips to make the most of these valuable partners.

Independent contractor or employee? Depending on what you ask them to do and how you want them to do it, the IRS might consider the person you thought was an independent contractor to be an employee. Misclassifying employees is a serious IRS offense, and if you're guilty of doing this (even inadvertently), you will not only have to pay taxes, but substantial penalties and fines, as well. Go to the IRS website to learn about the definitions (and differences) of independent contractors and employees to be sure you're not crossing the line.

Essentially, whether a person is classified as an employee or an independent contractor is based on how much "independence" they *actually* have. In general, an individual is an independent contractor if the employer has the right to control or direct only the *result* of the work and not what or how the work gets done. The IRS uses three tests to assess a worker's independence.

1—Behavioral test. Do you tell the worker what to do every day? Does the company control or have the right to control what the worker does and how the worker does their job? If you control the method used to complete the job, require certain hours be worked or specific tools be used then it's more likely the IRS would consider the worker to be an employee.

This doesn't mean you can't discuss what you want done on the project you're outsourcing or ask for progress updates—but you cannot restrict the hours the person works or where the work should be done. It's often best to have the work performed away from your place of business.

2—Financial test. Are the business aspects of the worker's job controlled by the payer (employer)? These include things like how worker is paid, whether expenses are reimbursed, who provides tools/supplies, etc. Should you pay your independent contractors mileage expenses? What about other expenses? Independent contractors usually pay their own expenses from gross receipts or revenues, or bundle the expenses into the overall project cost. However, many businesses do reimburse their independent contractors for mileage and other expenses. Paying expenses does not automatically mean misclassification. The IRS looks at the entirety of the employer/worker relationship. That said, you shouldn't offer to pay for materials, such as supplies, mailing tools, etc. The independent contractor should provide that on their own.

3—Relationship test. Are there written contracts or employee-type benefits (i.e. pension plan, insurance, vacation pay, etc.)? Will the relationship continue beyond the scope of the project, and is the work performed a key aspect of the business? Obviously, if you offer benefits, the worker should be classified as an employee. You need to make it clear the relationship is on a project-by-project basis or is temporary by putting exact wording to that effect in the employer/independent contract along with a specific end date. You can always draw up another agreement if the project is not completed by the stated date.

If you are concerned about classification, talk to your accountant or file Form SS-8 with the IRS. The IRS will analyze assess your situation and make an official decision on the worker's status. Remember, for every independent contractor who earns more than $600 from your company, you'll need to issue a 1099 to the IRS, and the contractor will need to fill out a W-9 form.

RESOURCES

Fiverr: https://www.fiverr.com/

99Designs: https://99designs.com/

Upwork: https://www.upwork.com/

Guru: https://www.guru.com/

Freelancer: https://www.freelancer.com/?t=h&utm_ expid=294858-538.FzfNAmBBSgWcClvukm10Iw.1&utm_ referrer=https%3A%2F%2Fwww.freelancer.com%2F

IRS definition of independent contractor: https://www.irs.gov/ businesses/small-businesses-self-employed/independent-contractor-self-employed-or-employee

Form SS-8: https://www.irs.gov/pub/irs-pdf/fss8.pdf

HACK 83

HOW TO MANAGE A VIRTUAL WORKFORCE

THE VERY NATURE OF team work has profoundly changed in the digital age. Most small businesses are no longer centralized in one location, but instead have employees and freelancers working from places all around the country—and the world. This is good news because your company can build a virtual team from the best resources anywhere on Earth.

This trend is also supported by local team members who want the convenience of sometimes working from home. For small business owners, this reduces the cost of physical office space, and all the additional expenses that are associated with it (utilities bills, for instance).

However, working virtually can also come at a cost. Without face-t0-face interaction, it becomes more difficult to build a cohesive team that can effectively work together. The isolation of a virtual employee from the business and culture is very real, and needs to be specifically addressed. In addition, employees are pressured by easy access to technology to work more hours, regardless of the time of day. While small business owners may see this as a positive trend, it does lead to increased burnout of team members.

To build a virtual team, a new style of management is required to maximize the performance of these virtual employees. You need to:

1—Specifically define goals and processes that can be tracked by everyone. Document the metrics that will define objectively what success for that employee looks like. This is particularly important for employees who can't be "seen" every day or where there is not regular one-on-one contact. For salespeople, it's easy to use their quota as the goal, but for customer service or development employees, it is can be more difficult to come up with measurable objectives. For virtual employees, these specific targets need to be reviewed monthly.

2—Provide the hardware to work remotely. Virtual employees may need additional solutions that office-bound employees do not have. This includes a webcam, smartphone, tablet and reliable remote access to all secure office applications.

3—Provide collaboration tools. Teams typically collaborate best with face-to-face meetings, not just via email. When this is not possible, use collaboration tools like Microsoft Office 365. These tools allow team members to work together, share versions, and leave comments. Chat apps like Slack or Microsoft Teams that integrate with business applications can help build conversation and camaraderie when team members are not in the same physical location. In a sense, it creates a virtual "water cooler" as an informal "location" to talk.

4—Check in with the employee by phone or video chat every other day. Texts, chat or email are effective for some tasks, but they don't establish the personal connection that is required for teamwork. Video calls will "force" the manager/owner to focus on being with that employee virtually.

5—Set up in-person meetings at least twice a year (three or four times is even better). There is nothing that can replace in-person meetings for establishing a solid working relationship. Once this takes place, it is easier to use virtual collaboration tools productively. Make sure these meetings include some type of social activity, such as sharing a meal to learn more about the whole person.

6—Over-communicate. Commit to a timetable of giving more feedback to a virtual employee than anyone who works in the same office. Remember, working outside the office can be an isolating experience where the employee does not really know what people think of the quality of their work. This focus will ensure they know they have your attention, and is more likely to keep them productive. It will also identify any conflicts early on, which are harder to detect when people are not physically together.

7—Make them part of the company. You need to think about how you extend your company's culture outside a physical location, especially if you have both in-person and virtual employees. Just including them on a conference call while everyone else is in the room is not optimal. Be sure to include them in monthly virtual events where they can participate as if they were there.

Remember, not every employee can be effective virtually. They need to have a lot of "self-awareness". This includes being a self-starter, self-motivated, self-disciplined, and mostly self-sufficient.

HACK 84

HOW TO MANAGE MILLENNIALS

By Alexandra Levit, Author, Speaker & Consultant

FOR MANY SMALL BUSINESS owners, onboarding and managing millennial employees is a challenge. Here is where to start.

1—Make a Solid First Impression. Go out of your way to get new millennial hires started on the right foot. Actively communicate with them between the offer and start date, and have their materials ready when they arrive. Don't leave them to their own devices, but get them immediately started on a project. Be proactive in understanding their unique capabilities. Take each employee to lunch or coffee, inquire about their dreams and aspirations, and tell them you genuinely care about their success. Emphasize collaboration in creating assignments for them, asking for their input and allowing them to be creative within certain boundaries. If they're getting their work done, be flexible in how you allow them to do it.

2—Offer a Crash Course on Your Culture. Educate new millennial hires about the ins and outs of your business: policies, standard operating procedures, and the unwritten rules. Make sure they understand what a good work ethic looks like in your organization. Direct their enthusiasm and energy into projects that allow them to make a valuable contribution. Guide them in networking around the system, providing coaching opportunities with star employees who are experts in various areas, and making a list of "go to" individuals who can provide support.

3—Practice Project-Based Mentorship. At its core, project-based mentorship puts employee development into the hands of many instead of being centered on a very busy business owner or supervisor. Each millennial has the opportunity to work on assignments with a diverse group of team members, all of whom are aware of their strengths and goals. In the context of the individual project, millennials may be placed in situations that are out of their comfort zones, and mentored actively on appropriate preparation, actions, and behaviors. Rather than allowing millennials to fail spectacularly, damaging their confidence, this form of shadowing facilitates small interventions to change unproductive habits now that might have negative consequences down the road.

4—Facilitate Leadership Experience. Small businesses can benefit by providing leadership opportunities outside of formal job titles so millennial employees can master decision making and problem solving. According to a *Deloitte Millennial Leadership* survey, millennials want to accelerate their development through cross-functional projects and increased interactions with the business owner. Millennials also value the apprenticeship model, in which they are allowed to work alongside business owners or managers during a typical project or atypical crisis situation. Apprenticeship is beneficial in anchoring new and soon-to-be millennial leaders in tangible responsibilities and real-world scenarios with reduced risk.

5—Provide Real-Time Feedback. Performance feedback must no longer be relegated to the semi-annual review or two-day management training seminar. Instead, you must provide real-time feedback on the experience you are creating for your millennial employees. For instance, you and your managers can send your staff a weekly survey that asks three simple questions: 1) Do you have the opportunity to play to your strengths every day? 2) Do your colleagues understand what quality work is? 3) Do you understand what is expected of you at work? The availability of low cost survey technology and the willingness of millennials to rate their own experiences makes it easy to quickly guide them in the right direction. You might also consider using an app like Slack or implementing an on-demand assessment system that limits responses to 140 characters. Millennials are accustomed to communicating via text, Twitter, and Instagram, so they respond well to the short-format, and they also value that responses can be collated into a performance dashboard through which they can track their career growth and progress.

Alexandra Levit specializes in helping organizations recruit, develop, and retain the best millennial employees.

RESOURCE

Alexandra Levit: http://www.alexandralevit.com/

HACK 85

HOW TO BRING THE CREATIVE OUT OF YOUR TEAM

By Laura Moncrieffe, Bamboo Worldwide

WHEN YOU'RE BUSY in the day-to-day of working *in* your business, it's hard to find time to step away to work *on* your business, to dream up ways to keep it fresh and relevant. To really get ahead, you need to leverage everyone on your team to be collecting new ideas and inspiration. Is your company's team equipped to conceptualize and implement these new ideas?

The answer for many small businesses will be, "No". Sure, you're staffed to run your business smoothly and efficiently, and you possess an entrepreneurial spirit to make things happen. But having a team with innovator skills, ready to identify ways to move your business forward, is a different apple altogether. If you truly want to build a team of problem solvers, you first have to ask yourself if you are ready to give up creative control.

Yes, that's right. In order to enable creative collaboration within your team, you must first let go of your creative control. If you are not ready to let go, then this hack will be a waste of time—and you can continue as you are, because a team that is ready to innovate together won't flourish under your leadership.

Business leaders often assume (negatively, I might add) their employees want the same solutions they find valuable, simply because they are the boss and no one verbally disagrees with them (in public, anyway.) Guess what? Employees won't fully incorporate your ideas into the organization if they don't also see them as valuable. A business won't change just because the leader wants it to. Sure, they might implement your policies, but they won't do it with the emotional ownership you need them to have for the change to stick.

Here's the kicker—you could all be aligned to the same goal, but you might tackle it in ways that are painful for each other. Therein lies the stumbling block with not giving up creative control. To move forward and solve problems effectively and creatively as a business, it's not about being in control of the innovative solutions. The key is about championing a team rich in diverse creative styles—and appreciating those differences.

Creativity = your value system

Have you ever heard your colleagues get excited about an idea and you're thinking, "I don't understand what all the 'hubbub' is about?" That's because your creative style determines your perspective of what you deem a great idea—one that you would be willing to support or pursue. A great idea is a matter of perspective, and that perspective changes with each team member. As individuals, we solve problems, and agree to implement changes, based on a personal value system we think leads to the biggest opportunities—and these "values" and "opportunities" are different for each person. Again, just because you are the leader does not mean your team will accept your "value system" when it comes to creative solutions.

Perceptions about you and your ideas happen every day. Those perceptions are based on your creative style, so not everyone will share them. And although some of the perceptions will be negative, that actually can be a positive cue that you have a creative counterpoint on your team, which is a huge asset if you choose to accept it!

What is a creative counterpoint? A creative counterpoint is someone who has a different value system when it comes to the criteria that makes an idea successful. They can help point out the gaps or red flags in your solution because they see success from a different perspective.

Finding your creative counterpoint is easy—just pinpoint someone who approaches problem solving in a different way than you do. Not just slightly different, but markedly different.

Pro Tips:

» A diversity of creative styles is best, even though it may be painful at times

» Know the creative 'value system' of your collective team, and how it is similar or different from your own

» Hiring your creative clone is a no-no

» Hiring your creative counterpoint is a plus

» Collaboration, not a top-down mandate, is key

» Try to understand the perspective of others

» Leaders don't have to create the change, but they must help champion it

Laura Moncrieffe has helped guide global marquee brands in their innovation and new product development initiatives for the past 25 years.

RESOURCE

Bamboo Worldwide: http://www.bambooworldwide.com/

HACK 86

HOW TO SURVIVE LOSING YOUR BEST EMPLOYEE (OR FREELANCER)

EVERY SMALL BUSINESS EXPERIENCES turnover. It can be very painful, especially when a long-time favorite employee resigns. Often, the owner has built the company with this employee for many years. They have trusted and relied on them—and now they are leaving. It can leave you feeling empty and alone.

So, how can a small business owner better prepare for this situation?

1—Don't being angry. It is critical to stop being mad or taking it personally. Every employee must do what is best for them. You must always understand this.

2—Prepare monthly. Regularly talk to these key people, and find out if their career goals still match the company's goals. Where do they intersect? This is a better question than simply asking the employee, "Are you still happy here?" Unfortunately, the employee often will not tell the whole truth, or may now know the answer until they are offered another opportunity.

3—Prepare quarterly. Think about who would replace each key person in the company if that employee left next week. This type of succession planning is critical to keeping the business moving forward when a key employee quits. This is especially important in the sales area.

Smart people move on. Company cultures change. As hard as this might be for you to accept, it is a stark reality. Hopefully, your business can evolve as employees come and go.

HACK 87

HOW TO APPRAISE/REVIEW EMPLOYEE PERFORMANCE

By Robin Kreitner, HR Professional

MOST EMPLOYEES AND THEIR bosses (whether that's you—or your managers) dread the performance appraisal process.

Employees feel they have no control in the performance review discussion. Their managers get to comment and rate them, which they feel is subjective. They don't believe they have an opportunity to disagree— and if they do write a rebuttal in the small space on the review form, they often think they'll be retaliated against by the person who conducted the review. Typically, the evaluation form is completed prior to the meeting between manager and employee, reinforcing the employee's view that there is no point in contradicting the boss. They don't want to be viewed as being confrontational.

Bosses don't like the performance review process either. They view it as just another cumbersome annoying requirement of being the boss—just another form to complete. They assume the discussion with the employee will be a struggle, and that the employee will undoubtedly think they are a better performer than the manager thinks. To get around the battle with the employee, the manager often rates the employee better on the form than reality dictates.

So, why even do a performance appraisal? Good question. According to SHRM (Society for Human Resources Management), 72% of companies conduct annual performance evaluations, and only 2% of employees say their companies get an "A" in performance management.

That said, when done well, the review process can have a positive impact on your business in several ways. It can make your team feel valued. The appraisal is an opportunity to provide and receive feedback on what is working well, and what can be improved. It's an opportunity to set new goals for the individual, and to communicate goals for the business, and how the employee can impact those goals. A discussion can also assess the training needs and desires of the employee and team, which could be useful during budget preparation.

If this sounds like it would be useful to have these types of conversation more than once per year, you're right. Companies are experimenting with doing less formal, but still required appraisal meetings quarterly rather than annually.

However often you appraise employees, following these common-sense steps will help ensure the meeting is useful and constructive:

» Use this opportunity as a communications tool. Avoid the tendency to do all the talking.

» Be prepared going into the meeting with the employee. Schedule the meeting in advance, and organize your thoughts so the conversation is clear and easy to follow.

» Start with positive comments about the employee's work. Use specific examples. If it is necessary to give criticism, be constructive. Use recent examples. Do not bring up an error from four months ago that has not been brought up before. Employees should never be totally caught off guard about their poor performances being brought up in a review discussion.

» Meet in private, and do not share performance feedback with other people in the department or company who do not have a need to know.

» Ask the employee how they would rate themselves. Perhaps even have them complete the same form you are required to complete prior to your meeting. This leads to a natural conversation as you compare the self-evaluation to the one you completed. Ask how they perceive they can improve in the areas of performance which are challenging.

» Listen and respond honestly. If their answer is they need the company to invest $100,000 in systems and training and that is not realistic, say so and regroup. Have the employee commit to the realistic steps they are going to take to improve.

» It is better to not confuse a salary discussion with an appraisal discussion. Keep the topics separate.

» Stay positive and unemotional. You are setting the tone.

Remember the goal of your meeting is to have a conversation around performance which will motivate and encourage your employees to move toward meeting the goals of your business.

Robin Kreitner is an HR professional with more than 30-years of experience.

RESOURCE
SHRM: https://www.shrm.org/

HACK 88

HOW AND WHEN TO FIRE AN EMPLOYEE

By Robin Kreitner, HR Professional

FIRING AN EMPLOYEE IS stressful for both parties involved. Obviously, it isn't fun for the person being fired. However, it is not easy for the person doing the firing either. Few people take pleasure out of telling someone bad news. Even if you think there is proper cause for termination, the employee usually does not believe they are actually going to be fired.

Of course, there are some reasons which warrant immediate termination. Some reasons of gross misconduct include: fighting or threatening violence in the workplace, theft, falsification of records, job abandonment, possession of dangerous materials such as firearms or explosives, possession or use of illegal drugs while on the job. You should include a list of all the reasons for gross misconduct and lesser disciplinary actions in a company personnel manual/employee handbook or a document which is given to and signed by each new employee.

It is important to remember every former employee (and job candidate, for that matter) is a future customer who has family and friends they will tell about how they were treated. Treating the employee kindly, in a humane manner, is not only the right thing to do, it will make this difficult task easier for you, and perhaps most important, it will be more likely to keep you and your company away from potential costly legal consequences. Here are some pointers to make a bad situation go more smoothly:

1—Be certain and be prepared. Don't rush into anything—even when you think there is gross misconduct. Be certain you have the facts and that, if questioned, you have adequate proof. Know your facts and what you are going to say. Review briefly what has led to the decision to terminate. Keep it simple and factual. Know if a company policy exists, and how similar infractions have been handled in the past. *Consistency* is crucial to protect against potential legal action.

2—Privacy. Meet with the employee in private, out of earshot and sight of other employees. Set aside at least 20 to 30 minutes to be sure you have enough time to explain the situation and answer questions.

3—Document and communicate. If the reason isn't gross misconduct, be sure the proper guidelines and procedures for steps of disciplinary action have taken place, and have been documented and communicated to the employee. There shouldn't be any surprises.

4—Don't go it alone. If you have a Human Resources department or person, check with them and follow their instructions. If your company doesn't have a HR department, is there someone you can consult with, such as an attorney or HR consultant? Don't make this important decision on your own.

5—Have a checklist. Do you need to have the employee return company property (computer, phone, keys, important documents)? Know ahead of time what you need to do to wrap-up the employment relationship. Be prepared to discuss how and when the employee will receive their final paycheck, what will happen with their vacation or personal time not yet taken, health benefit continuation (COBRA paperwork if it pertains to your company is required to be given to the departing employee), employment references, etc.

6—Safety. Is there any possibility the employee will be so angry they could become a possible danger to you or other employees? Having a witness with you not only provides safety in numbers, but it lessens the potential of the employee claiming harassment, other illegal behavior or something as simple as reporting you said something you didn't.

7—Don't argue and get defensive. Remember this is not about you. At the end of the day you still have a job, and don't have to tell a loved one you are no longer employed. Stay calm, use your "indoor" voice, be empathetic and sympathetic. Say something like, "I understand you are upset and I want to answer your questions. But I want you to understand the decision has been made and will not be changing." Let the employee vent for a reasonable period of time.

8—Wish them well. At the end of the conversation, shake hands and wish the person well. Say, "I'm sorry this didn't work out the way you would have liked, but I wish you well in your future endeavors." Don't lecture or offer advice. The outgoing employee doesn't want to hear it, and it isn't kind or helpful. It might make you feel better but again, this is not about you.

Robin Kreitner is an HR professional with more than 30-years of experience.

HACK 89

HOW TO HANDLE AN UNEMPLOYMENT HEARING

By Zane Smith, Attorney, Zane Smith & Associates

MOST EMPLOYERS WILL BE faced with a situation where they have to let go of employees. Here are five considerations for employers faced with a terminated employee making claims for unemployment benefits.

1—Know your state's employment laws. Most states in the U.S. are at-will employment states, meaning employees can be terminated by employers for any reason, and without warning. As long as the employee is not within a protected class (race, color, religion, national origin, sex, disability, and familial status), and that class protection is not the basis for the termination, the employer can terminate the employee without giving a reason. In states that do not have at-will employment, you must prove just cause for terminating the employee. Generally, employees who are out of work through no fault of their own are eligible for unemployment benefits.

2—Document the decision-making process. Regardless of the state's at-will employment status, when terminating an employee, you should always record the date, time, and place of the termination, and if possible you should always have a witness. If the employee is terminated for cause, meaning you have a reason for terminating them (they're stealing from you, they're late too many times, they're not performing at the level expected), this too must be documented in a way that will preserve the record and the supporting reason for the termination. (See Hack #89.) An employee seeking unemployment benefits is required to comply with all the employee handbook rules of termination in order to make an unemployment claim. If the employee fails to comply with all their post-employment obligations, make sure that paperwork is also provided to the unemployment agency so the employee's action can be taken into consideration. These records will be absolutely essential in prevailing in an unemployment hearing.

3—Request a hearing if... The unemployment claim usually begins with a letter from the local state government agency stating that your former employee filed a claim for unemployment benefits. If, in fact, they are entitled to those benefits, you need do nothing. Their benefits will be paid by the state. Usually the employer is not required to make direct payments to an employee who files a claim. However, there will usually be a direct adverse effect on the premiums or contributions required by the employer into the agency's unemployment fund based on the number of claims the employer has. Thus, if you feel your employee's claim for unemployment benefits is baseless then you should request a hearing.

4—Know the unemployment hearing process. In an unemployment hearing, there is a representative from the unemployment agency, the employee, employer, and or any number of witnesses involved. Often, these hearings are conducted by telephone. If you feel it's important to present evidence in a visual way, then request an in-person hearing. Otherwise, you can provide a response to the claim in written form, provide supporting documentation, and wait for the decision.

5—Appeal—only if it's a good business decision. Most times, if you have a valid reason for terminating an employee for cause, the employee's unemployment application will be denied. States have different rules, but in general, once the employee's application for unemployment benefits is denied, those benefits can only be resurrected if the employee goes through an appeals process with the state or local court system. While that appeals process is also available to the employer, you must take into account the cost of litigation versus the risk of increased unemployment contributions. This is purely a business decision.

In summary, if you feel the employee is not entitled to unemployment benefits, you should contest them, and your chances of are winning significantly increased if you can provide witnesses and documentation to support the decision to fire the employee for cause.

Zane Smith has been practicing law for over 35 years.

RESOURCE

Zane Smith: www.zanesmith.com

HACK 90

HOW TO SET UP THE BEST ORGANIZATION CHART

MOST SMALL BUSINESS OWNERS do not have a traditional hierarchical reporting structure for their companies. This is typically bad news since the organization looks like a hub and spoke system. In this set up, all the decision making is centralized and every important conversation is one on one with the owner. There is also no standardization of tasks. While this may feed the owner's ego, it does nothing to build a strong, motivated and leveraged company.

As the business grows, a more bureaucratic structure usually develops, with a stricter hierarchy since the owner can't be everywhere. Clear definitions of the responsibilities for each functional job are documented. There is a respect for merit, but also politics and personal relationships play an influential role here. This is where a company culture starts to take shape independent from the small business owner.

In this organization, there are strict management and individual contributor levels. The management layer works directly with the owner or CEO of the company. As the organization grows, there can be many layers of top-down decision making.

This can work well for organizations that require quick command and control decisions, but it creates few leaders and more followers. All strategic decision-making is done at the top. Unfortunately, over time, this strict structure can stifle innovation and creativity in rapidly changing markets. The key to creating a strong hierarchical organization is to task each manager with setting departmental goals within the company's overall mission. They may work with the owner on what needs to be accomplished, but they are responsible for how it will be achieved. As a result, they are given their own budget and hiring authority for their team.

For hierarchical organizations to be effective, each person on the chart needs to be evaluated quarterly within their jobs, their impact on achieving these specific goals, and how they contribute to the overall company. Weak team members can bring down a department or an entire company. In truly effective businesses, people who do not perform have no place to hide and are ushered out. Team members need to be cross-trained to fill in for employees who leave.

HOW TO DECIDE ON THE RIGHT STRUCTURE FOR YOUR SMALL BUSINESS.

One size does not fit all. It is critical to align your company's strategy and market environment with an organizational structure that will allow it to optimally operate. If the business is producing low-cost and high-volume products, the traditional hierarchical organization can be very successful. If the company depends on constant innovation in a volatile marketplace, then it may not be effective. For a small organization, too many specialized silos could paralyze it. If the company grows to greater than 15 people, there are economies of scale by maintaining specialized departments with more decentralized decision making. An organization with strict controls is needed if the company is working in highly-regulated industries, such as health care, insurance or finance.

As an organization grows, it will shift organization structure types. There are a lot of tools, such as Organimi to help small business owners create, maintain and share their organization charts.

RESOURCE
Organimi: http://www.organimi.com/

CUSTOMER EXPERIENCE HACKS

HACK 91

HOW TO PERSONALIZE SERVICE TO YOUR CUSTOMERS

TODAY'S CONSUMERS WANT—AND expect—the personal touch when they do business with you. Luckily, for small business owners, offering personalized service is one area where they can shine.

Whether you're a retailer or restaurant owner serving customers in person, or a B2B business with a devoted call center, here are some tactics you and your employees can use to personalize your customers' experiences.

1—Address them by name. Learn the names of your loyal and frequent customers so you and your employees can greet them by name. You should also use your customers' names when you communicate with them, whether that's via direct mail, email newsletters or text messages.

2—Smile and make eye contact for more personalized customer service. This may sound obvious, but it's something too many front-line employees forget to do. As texting and social media replace face-to-face communications, we're seeing more young, entry-level employees who lack basic social skills. Train your staff to greet all customers with a smile. And when they interact with them, make sure they look them straight in the eye.

3—Implement a loyalty program. Loyalty programs range from the simple (handing out paper punch cards) to spontaneously giving a regular customer a free dessert. But today's technology allows small business owners to step up their offerings by using digital loyalty programs such as Belly or LevelUp.

Digital loyalty programs do more than just offer rewards to your customers. They can gather data about customer behaviors, which helps you market to customers in more personalized ways. Using these programs, you can create personalized marketing messages based on the specific products or services your customers are interested in.

4—Offer multiple customer service channels. Not all customers like to get help the same way. Some prefer talking via live chat, others would rather send an email, and still others want to talk to someone on the phone.

By providing multiple touchpoints for accessing customer service, you can allow customers to personalize their experience using whatever method they prefer.

5—Be human. At some point, we've all talked to a customer service rep who was just reciting rote answers off a script, making us feel they weren't really listening.

Some of us have also experienced customer service reps who chat with us while they're working on our issue. Something as simple as asking a customer how the weather is in their area, or if they've seen the latest "hot" movie helps humanize the experience.

6—Collect and share customer data. While you can jot down data on notepads, the best way to collect data on your customers is to use a reliable CRM system. These let you maintain detailed records about your customers and their previous interactions with your business. If your customer service employees can all access this information, they can then personalize interactions by referencing previous orders or past service issues.

7—Make recommendations. Steal a page from Amazon's book and use information about customers' past purchasing behaviors to recommend new products they might like. For instance, a retailer could make suggestions when customers visit the store, or send them an email or text message when new products come in that they might like.

If you sell products on your website, you can add a recommendation feature which offers suggestions for similar or complementary purchases to shoppers as they browse products or services, or put items in their carts.

RESOURCES

Belly: https://www.bellycard.com/

LevelUp: https://www.thelevelup.com/

HACK 92

HOW TO BE AN AUTHENTIC BUSINESS

CONSUMERS TODAY WANT to do business with companies they see as honest and authentic. Being perceived as "authentic" brings many advantages. Studies show most consumers would actually do something to "reward" a business they believe is authentic, including refer their friends and colleagues to the business and become more loyal customers themselves.

But what makes a business authentic in consumers' eyes? The quick answers are:

» Delivering on promises

» Providing "high quality" products or services

» Being socially- or environmentally-responsible

It's also important to:

1—Maintain a strong brand identity. As you grow, you need to make sure your brand's mission and vision statements (see Hack #1) are still relevant. Then make sure you and your team "live the brand" every day when you interact with customers, vendors and suppliers. in their interactions with customers.

2—Tell your story. How did your company start? What inspired you to become a small business owner? Did you take over a family-owned business or buy a business from a retiring owner? People love to buy from companies with a human-interest story behind them—and every business has one. Make sure you tell yours.

3—Show your personality. Authentic businesses aren't corporate or faceless. If appropriate, weave your passion for your business, how you got started, any big wins into your marketing materials.

4—Be active in your community. If you sell locally, your community could be the neighborhood your customers come from. If you sell nationally or globally, your community could be the larger group your customer base comes from, such as musicians or parents of young children. Show your community that you share their concerns—and you're working with them to make the world a better place. That might mean getting involved in or starting a "buy local" campaign to unite local merchants, or donating time and money to a global cause.

5—Deliver what you promise. As noted above, this is of primary importance to consumers. Honesty and integrity are vitally important to a business's authenticity. Make sure your products and services are top quality; provide guarantees to show you stand behind what you do. Monitor your business's presence on social media and online review sites (see Hacks #95 & #96) to make sure you're living up to your good reputation in the eyes of your customers. Respond to complaints quickly and with a willingness to resolve them.

HACK 93

HOW TO MAKE MORE MONEY FROM YOUR EXISTING CUSTOMERS

ONE OF THE EASIEST WAYS to grow your small business is to get more sales from your existing customer base. Here are 10 ways to increase profits by getting the maximum value from your current customers and clients.

1—Sell more. Are your best customers buying all your s products or services? Create a chart listing all your customers on one axis and your products on the other. Place an X where each customer is buying a given product. Use this chart to discover where your holes are. If they already trust your company, they will want to buy more things from you.

2—Incentivize greater usage. Encourage your customers to use your products or services more often. Offer loyalty programs (see Hack #100) or bonuses for repeat business to your best customers. This is especially true in industries where products are commodities or they can be easily sourced. Great examples of this are Amazon Prime and airline frequent flyer programs.

3—Communicate consistently. Use content marketing strategies to send customers useful information like articles and newsletters that are both educational and funny. This can be original advice or links to relevant articles. Keep in touch with your customers at least once a week using multiple mediums so you can be there when they are ready to buy.

4—Know your customers. Mine your data. Know what, when, and how much your customers buy monthly or annually. Invest time and money in knowing exactly how your customers think, what they like, what they dislike, and tailor offers to match. This data can be found in Google Analytics, your CRM system, your accounting programs or shopping cart system.

5—Know your ABCs. Separate your customers into A's, B's, and C's, according to their lifetime value to your company. Measure them based on purchases, referrals, and brand recognition. Come up with a strategy to move C's to B's and B's to A's.

6—Become the "go-to". Leverage your strategic alliances to connect your customers to other resources that can fill their needs and desires which are beyond the scope of your business. Your customers will view you as their "go-to-resource," which gives you an opportunity to go from being a vendor to a partner.

7—Show thanks frequently. Build customer loyalty by rewarding your customers beyond financial incentives. Call them to express your appreciation, or send a handwritten card. Post a thank you on their social media pages or feeds.

8—Make an exclusive club. In addition to recognition, people love to feel a sense of belonging. Create a membership group for your customers with special offers and privileges for members. Costco and Sam's Club do this very effectively.

9—Sell a subscription. Renewable products are ones that customers use and need to buy again. Harry's (razor blades) and Birchbox (cosmetics) are successful examples. This will ensure your business always has customers at the beginning of every month.

10—Just ask. Simply ask your customers what they want. They may not always be able to tell you directly, but it will start a dialogue that will eventually get you the information you need. This can be done easily through two to three question surveys using Survey Gizmo or SurveyMonkey.

RESOURCES

SurveyMonkey: https://www.surveymonkey.com/

SurveyGizmo: https://www.surveygizmo.com/

HACK 94

HOW TO GET A REFERRAL FROM YOUR CUSTOMERS

RATING AND REVIEW SITES are important tools for small business owners, but one of the most powerful customer attraction tactics you can use is an old-fashioned one—getting referrals from existing customers. Referral marketing is a low-cost (possibly no-cost) way to get highly-qualified leads. Here's how to start a referral marketing program in your small business.

1—**What type of referral are you looking for?** There are different levels of referrals. On the most basic level, you might ask a client to give you the name and email address or phone number of someone who might be interested in doing business with you. This is a fairly low-value referral. It's more valuable when a customer discusses your business with the potential referral, and can tell you they are interested in learning more. Finally, the highest level and most valuable referral would be a customer who actually introduces you to the referral, or arranges a meeting between the two (or three) of you. Depending on your needs and your industry, you might want to seek referrals on all these levels.

2—**Create a system.** The most important step is to systematize the referral process, ensuring that asking for referrals isn't just an afterthought, but something that's built into your sales cycle. For example, you may want to ask for a referral when you are invoicing the client for completing the job, or do it later as part of your post-sale follow-up. Create reminders within your email marketing system.

3—Timing is key. Through testing, you'll be able to discern the best time to request a referral and make it part of your sales and customer service process. It's important to ask for a referral when the customer is feeling positive about your company. If you unwittingly ask a frustrated or angry customer for a referral, your efforts can backfire—so make sure your timing is right.

4—Offer rewards. Receiving discounts or other promotions on your products and services are a great reward for customers who refer others to you. You could provide a reward simply for giving a referral, such as a 15% discount off the next purchase for providing a few names and emails, or make it contingent on the referral making a purchase, such as offer a free month's worth of services if they refer someone who becomes a customer.

5—Follow up. After not asking for referrals, the biggest mistake small business owners make is getting referrals and not following up on them. Build a timeline into your system so you follow up within two weeks of getting the referral. Otherwise, the prospect could forget about you, could buy what you sell somewhere else or could simply turn from a hot lead into a cold case.

HACK 95

HOW TO GET ONLINE REVIEWS FROM YOUR CUSTOMERS

R ATINGS AND REVIEWS from customers are key to driving new customers to your business. In fact, numerous surveys have shown consumers trust online reviews more than they trust recommendations from family and friends.

The more reviews you have on the ratings and review sites, the more reliable and trustworthy your business will seem to new customers.

But too many small business owners aren't doing everything they can to encourage online reviews. This can lead to consumers not learning about—or purposely avoiding—your business when the don't see it listed when they go to a review site.

So, how can you encourage customers to leave reviews? I say "encourage" here, because actively soliciting or requesting reviews is frowned upon by many review sites and providing incentives such as discounts or freebies in exchange for reviews can get you in trouble. Instead, try these steps.

1—Post signs in your store, restaurant or office. This is a simple, subtle (and inexpensive) way to tell customers your business is on review sites and that you'd love them to review you

Yelp, for instance, has downloadable "Find us on Yelp" banners you can print out as signage for your store window or point-of-sale counter.

2—Use receipts. On your receipts or restaurant checks say, "Like us? Review us on [list the review sites where you have a presence]."

Post sale (whether online or off), send a follow-up email making sure the customer is happy. Include a reminder about what review sites your business is on.

3—Spread the word. Put icons for the review sites where you have a presence in your print marketing materials, on your website (you can use the downloadable Yelp banners there), in your email signature and anywhere else you can think of. They serve as a constant reminder to review your business.

4—Make it easy. The key is to not ask your customers to do the heavy lifting. People will be more inclined to review your business, if it's not a hassle. Put clickable links on your site that go directly to the review site. For example, if your site says, "Like us? Review us on Yelp," make sure there's a clickable link right there.

One word of caution: Never (I mean never!) fake a review, or have friends and family write them. The review sites have formulas and algorithms (secret of course) they use to flush out fake reviews. The key to garnering good reviews is delivering on the promises you make—and being authentic while you do it.

HACK 96

HOW TO DEAL WITH NEGATIVE ONLINE REVIEWS

YOU CANNOT AFFORD TO ignore negative online reviews or ratings. Why? Consumers are reliant on reading reviews before spending a dime—in fact, surveys show about 90% of consumers admit their buying decisions are influenced by online reviews. That's great if your business generates positive reviews. But what if you have negative one? The bad news is 86% of consumers won't buy from a business with negative reviews. So, it's crucial you try to turn a negative review into a positive one. Here's how.

1—Take action. Monitor what customers are saying about your small business. You can set up a system internally or use a service that does it for you.

2—Don't get mad. Most people will react negatively to a negative review, but that's the worst thing you can do. Instead, apologize to the customer for what went wrong (remember, most times the customer is always right), explain you want to correct the situation, and then ask the customer to contact you—offline. Make sure you personalize your response to the situation—this is not the time for form letters.

3—Talk offline. Under no circumstances should you argue about a negative review in a public forum. Instead, tell the customer how to contact you offline, either by phone or email. Or, ask how you can get in touch with them

4—Don't argue, listen. When the customer contacts you, apologize again, and be empathetic about what happened. Let them explain the problem. Don't get defensive or make excuses.

5—Resolve the problem. Once you've heard the problem, ask the customer what they think a fair solution would be. This shows you're at least willing to listen—even if their idea of fair and yours are different. If their suggestion is within reason, try to accommodate their request.

6—Mean what you say. Once you agree to fixing the problem, fix it—quickly. You don't want to make a bad situation worse or compound the problem. Follow up with the customer to make sure they're happy.

7—Correct the record. If you think you've diffused the situation, ask the customer if they would remove the negative review. In some cases, it might be better to leave the negative review up, along with your response, an updated review from the customer explaining how you resolved the issue, and how happy they now are. This shows you value customers' feedback and will do what it takes to keep them happy. And consumers don't trust businesses with only positive reviews.

If the customer won't remove or change their negative review, you can contact the review website, but most sites won't remove a review unless it's libelous or defamatory. Read the site's Terms of Service and/or Content Guidelines to see if the review meets their criteria for offensiveness.

Before you dismiss all negative reviews, ask yourself if the customer was in any way justified for complaining. Bad reviews can help you, by highlighting any weak spots in your business.

And remember, your positive reviews will outweigh the negative ones, so encourage (but don't solicit) your customers and clients to post about their good experiences. (See Hack #95.)

How will you know when you receive a negative review? It's essential you monitor your ratings and reviews. Yes, it can be overwhelming to keep track of the numerous social media platforms, blogs, websites and traditional media where people could be talking about your business. Sign up for alerts from Google and Bing.

RESOURCES

Social Mention: http://www.socialmention.com/

Reputation Alert: https://www.networksolutions.com/online-marketing/online-reputation/index.jsp

Rankur: https://rankur.com/

Trackur: http://www.trackur.com/

HACK 97

HOW TO DEAL WITH AN ANGRY CUSTOMER

By Hillary Berman, Founder, Popcorn & Ice Cream & Author

EVEN THE BEST BUSINESSES sometimes have dissatisfied customers. Someone makes a mistake. Products don't ship on time. Circumstances beyond your control impact your ability to deliver as promised. Customers have unrealistic or incorrect expectations. The reasons are endless. No matter how hard you work to deliver a top-notch customer experience, infallible product or rave-worthy service, sometimes things simply go wrong.

No business owner likes angry customers. The truth is—customers don't like being angry either. The key to making even the most irate customer happy again is by reframing your thinking to view the situation as an opportunity rather than an annoyance—no matter who is at fault. Bad situations give you the ability to convert an unhappy customer into an advocate and gain invaluable feedback that helps your business continuously improve in the process.

Get customers smiling again with these customer service hacks—each a step toward lowering customer frustration:

1—Take a deep breath. It's natural to get defensive when an angry customer comes at you full bore. But nothing escalates a situation more than defensiveness or meeting fire with fire. Take a moment to take a deep breath and focus on resolution. You want customers to remember how you handled the situation above the issue that caused it to occur.

2—Say thank you. While angry customers' rants are often brutal and, thanks to social media, increasingly public, knowing a customer is unhappy is far better the alternative. When they stay silent, you suffer from negative comments they share with friends and inability to correct the situation so others don't suffer a similar outcome. Thank them for taking the time to share their frustrations with you and giving you the opportunity to make things right.

3—Say I'm sorry. When you apologize, you take ownership of the situation—regardless of who is at fault. Say "I'm sorry for the situation," "the misunderstanding," or "how you feel." Do this sincerely and without a "but" at the end of the sentence.

4—Ask questions. Often, angry customers simply want to be heard. In some cases, they aren't seeking compensation for their dissatisfaction, but rather the knowledge the company cares enough to listen. Start by asking for their perspective to get an understanding of why they're upset.

5—Make things right. In some cases, angry customers deserve a refund or a replacement. In others, a smile and sympathetic ear are all that is appropriate or necessary. Armed with the information you gathered by asking questions, address their specific frustrations rather than simply throw a generic "We're sorry, here's 10% off your next order" response at them.

6—Look for trends. Beyond the single customer situation, keep an eye out for patterns of issues or something notably concerning. Angry customer feedback provides some of the best insight for identifying issues and opportunities to improve your product, service or experience.

Hillary Berman is the founder of Popcorn & Ice Cream, a small business marketing consultancy in Washington, DC, and the author of Customer, LLC: The Small Business Guide to Customer Engagement & Marketing. *You can reach her at Hillary@popcorn-icecream.com.*

RESOURCE

Popcorn & Ice Cream: https://popcorn-icecream.com/

HACK 98

HOW TO GET RID OF TOXIC CUSTOMERS

ALL SMALL BUSINESSES have bad customers. But why should you accept that? There are times these customers become so toxic, keeping them financially hurts your company.

Toxic customers are often disrespectful to employees, driving them to quit. Or they impact staff morale because of their constant complaints. If customers end up costing you more to service than any profit they contribute to the bottom line, you should consider firing them. (Costs include the additional time it takes to address their complaints or other special considerations.).

So, how can you identify toxic customers? Here are some warning signs.

1—The company is no longer helping them. Admit it; these customers are wasting their money. They will eventually stop buying anyway if they don't see the value in your services.

2—The customer is disregarding advice. This can only end badly for your reputation, since eventually, they will blame you for their lack of success. This will lead to a dissatisfied customer, and could result in a bad review posted on social media.

3—The customer is not willing to pay your rates. Not getting paid what you're worth negatively impacts your bottom line. In addition, they may not be paying their bills on time, which affects your cash flow.

4—The customer asks the team to do something illegal or unethical. Regardless of what they promise to pay, if the customer has behaved unethically or illegally, seek HR or legal advice, and terminate the relationship immediately.

5—The customer has behaved inappropriately toward one of your employees. This is another case where HR or legal advice is needed. Accepting this type of behavior reflects poorly on you, the business owner, and says a lot about what type of behavior you will tolerate.

How and when to fire toxic customers

Frequently, toxic customers are a large part of your revenue, because they can't work with other companies. As a result, you need to fire them "carefully", by creating a termination plan, so losing them does not severely impact your company.

The first step is to identify potential prospects that can replace the problem customer. Start phasing out the "fired" customer when these additional clients come on board. Next, show the toxic customers other "options for their needs" by telling them they would be happier with another business (even a competitor). Finally, set an internal date for when you'll no longer be willing to do business with them.

After the toxic customer is fired, it is also important not to permit your employees to discuss them. This is just gossip, and serves no business purpose. And, there's always the danger of this information getting back to the customers, especially in our social media world.

HACK 99

HOW TO IMPROVE CUSTOMER EXPERIENCE

CUSTOMER SERVICE HAS morphed into what we now call "customer experience" (CX for short). CX cover every "touchpoint" where customers interact with your business, from visiting your website to buying your products or contracting for your services, from post-purchase follow-up to customer service interactions.

That's a lot of customer interactions, which can make it a bit difficult to create extraordinary customer experiences for your clients and customers?

First, think about the specific reasons your customers like doing business with you. What are the advantages of working with your company, instead of your competitors? Are these parts of your business where you're already offering excellent CX? What can you learn from how you execute there?

You can't tackle all customer touchpoints at one time, so consider starting with these four ways to improve your CX:

1—Marketing segmentation. You should be collecting data about your customers every time they do business with you. Then, select promotions and offers to send them, based on the data you have. Start by segmenting them into general demographic groups, such as age, gender and where they live. The more information you collect, the more you'll be able to personalize your marketing messages to them.

2—Cement relationships. When you send customers personalized marketing messages, whether via email, text or off-line direct marketing, you create a positive impression of your business. Personalizing those messages makes customers feel you're paying attention to their habits, that you care about them, what they buy, and how they shop. You'll also discover which marketing messages they're most responsive to—which builds a bond between you, solidifying the relationship they have with your business.

3—Seek their input. Everyone wants to believe their opinions matter—and you customers are no exception. Monitor what they say about you on social media (see Hack #96)—and, whenever possible, enact their ideas and suggestions. Be proactive and conduct surveys about all aspects of your business, including customer experience. This gives your customers the opportunity to formally provide feedback, and again shows them you care about what they think.

4—Make it personal. If a customer calls your business's customer service department, will they be greeted by name? If the customer service rep is able to pull up their account, past purchasing history and other personalized information, they can do that. Store your customer data in the cloud, so it's easy to access customers' previous interactions and purchases.

HACK 100

HOW TO GENERATE CUSTOMER LOYALTY

CUSTOMERS EXPECT MORE from businesses these days—they want to be rewarded for spending their hard-earned money with you. And we're not talking those old buy-12-get-one-free programs. For many consumers those rewards come from joining a customer loyalty program. In fact, surveys show the average American household has memberships in 29 loyalty programs.

From the business owner's point of view, loyalty programs work—consumers who belong to them generate 12-18% more incremental revenue growth per year.

How do you craft an effective customer loyalty program? Consumers are looking for programs that feature:

1—Offers. Consumers are loyal to brands that give them discounts, gift cards and special offers to reward their loyalty. If you do this, make sure you track which offers get the best results and generate the most profits.

2—Personalization. Personalized products are increasingly in-demand today. Offer loyalty program members free customization, such as engraving a product or special ordering custom-color sneakers.

3—Innovation. Many consumers want to do business with companies that offer new experiences, products or services, and sell the "latest" products. Create special experiences for your loyalty program members, such as VIP sales, early access to sales or early access to new products.

4—Celebrities. Partnering with "social influencers" or celebrities, such as popular bloggers or YouTube personalities drives loyalty in some consumers.

5—Family and Friends. Consumers are loyal to companies their families and friends do business with. Consider offering loyalty program members a reward for getting friends or family to sign up, too.

6—Participation. Many consumers are loyal to businesses that involve them in designing or creating new products or services. Ask your "VIP" customers to help choose which new products your store will carry or let them weigh in on new services.

Once you create a customer loyalty program, you can't just set it and forget it. It's crucial to monitor your ROI. Examine all the metrics to determine whether your investment in a loyalty program is paying off. Assess the costs of your retail loyalty program, both in terms of the fees for the program and the costs. If it's not working for you as well as you'd hoped, try cutting out some parts of the program or switch some of the rewards for ones that cost less. Rather than giving something away for free, offer value-added rewards instead.

Monitor your competitors' programs. Is there something missing from their loyalty offerings you can offer? How can you differentiate your retail loyalty program from theirs? Promote your loyalty program in all your marketing efforts, including making sure your staff brings it up when checking people out.

Finally, make sure your loyalty program has a mobile component. There are a number of digital loyalty programs to help small businesses, including Belly, Loyalzoo and Perka. These programs let you capture customer data, such as what they buy and what promotions they respond to, which makes it easier to create customized marketing messages for them.

RESOURCES

Belly: https://www.bellycard.com/

Loyalzoo: https://www.loyalzoo.com/

Perka: https://www.perka.com/

SHARE YOUR FAVORITE HACK!

www.yoursmallbizhacks.com

65752652R00172

Made in the USA
Middletown, DE
03 March 2018